PIANO • VOCAL • GUITAR

IRISH PUB SONGS

ISBN: 978-1-4234-1136-9

HAL•LEONARD®
CORPORATION

7777 W. BLUEMOUND RD. P.O. BOX 13819 MILWAUKEE, WI 53213

In Australia contact:
Hal Leonard Australia Pty. Ltd.
4 Lentara Court
Cheltenham, Victoria, 3192 Australia
Email: ausadmin@halleonard.com

Visit Hal Leonard Online at
www.halleonard.com

Piano • Vocal • Guitar

Irish Pub Songs

5 ALL FOR ME GROG

6 ARThUR McBRIDE

9 BLACK VELVET BAND

14 BRENNAN ON THE MOOR

16 A BUNCH OF THYME

18 CLIFFS OF DONEEN

24 DANNY BOY

26 DICEY REILLY

28 DO YOU WANT YOUR OLD LOBBY

32 THE FIELDS OF ATHENRY

21 FINNEGAN'S WAKE

36 THE GERMAN CLOCKWINDER

39 HILLS OF CONNEMARA

40 THE HUMOUR IS ON ME NOW

42 I NEVER WILL MARRY

44 I'M A ROVER AND SELDOM SOBER

46 THE IRISH ROVER

48 ISN'T IT GRAND, BOYS?

54 JOHNSON'S MOTOR CAR

56 JUG OF PUNCH

58 THE JUICE OF THE BARLEY

60 LEAVING OF LIVERPOOL

62 MACNAMARA'S BAND

64 MUIRSHEEN DURKIN

51 A NATION ONCE AGAIN

68 NORA

74 THE PARTING GLASS

71 QUARE BUNGLE RYE

76 THE RARE OULD TIMES

79 THE RISING OF THE MOON

82 THE ROSE OF TRALEE

85 ROYAL CANAL

88 SEVEN DRUNKEN NIGHTS

94 SPANCIL HILL

96 THE STONE OUTSIDE DAN MURPHY'S DOOR

91 TWENTY-ONE YEARS

100 THE WAXIES DARGLE

103 WHISKEY, YOU'RE THE DEVIL

106 WHISKEY IN THE JAR

109 WILD ROVER

ALL FOR ME GROG

Traditional Irish Folk Song

ARTHUR McBRIDE

Traditional Irish Folk Song

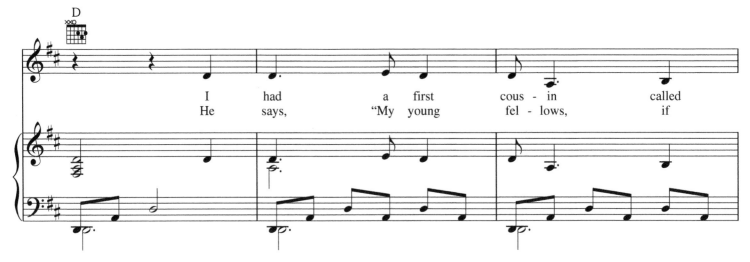

I had a first cous - in called
He says, "My young fel - lows, if

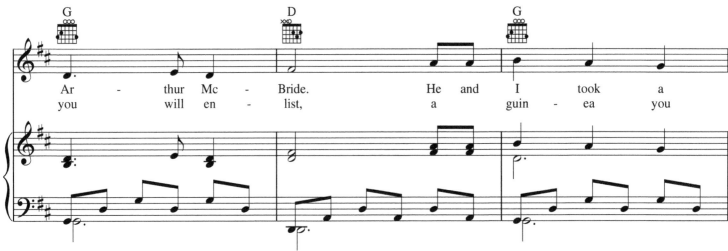

Ar - thur Mc - Bride. He and I took a
you will en - list, a guin - ea you

stroll down _____ by the sea - side, a -
quick - ly shall have in your ___ fist. Be -

seek - ing good for - tune and what might be -
sides _____ a crown for to kick up the

tide, 'twas just as the day was a -
dust, and drink as the king's health in the

dawn - ing. Then af - ter
morn - ing." Had we been such

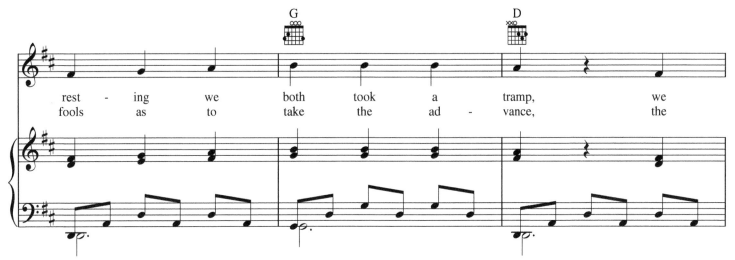

rest - ing we both took a tramp, we
fools as to take the ad - vance, the

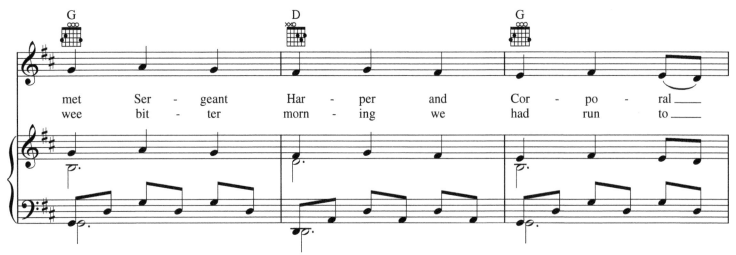

met Ser - geant Har - per and Cor - po - ral ___
wee bit - ter morn - ing we had run to ___

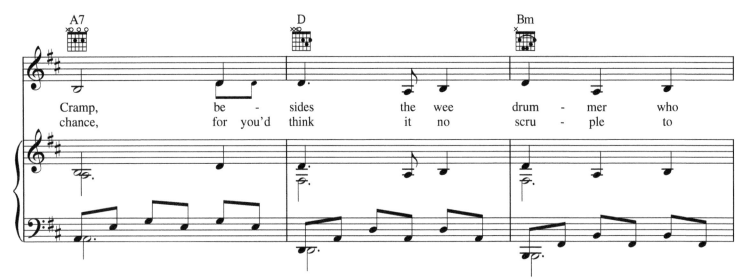

Cramp, be - sides the wee drum - mer who
chance, for you'd think it no scru - ple to

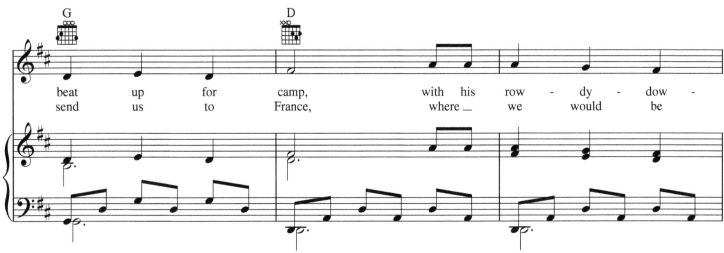

beat up for camp, with his row - dy - dow -
send us to France, where ___ we would be

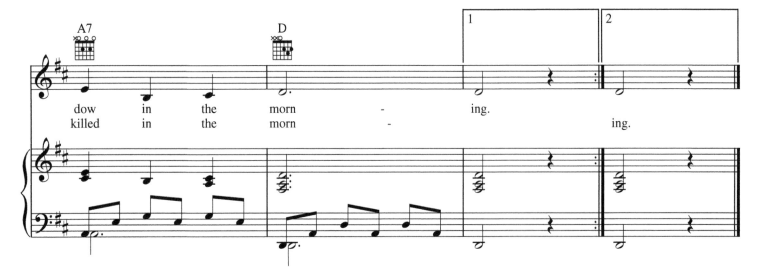

dow in the morn - ing.
killed in the morn - ing.

BLACK VELVET BAND

Traditional Irish Folk Song

Lyrically

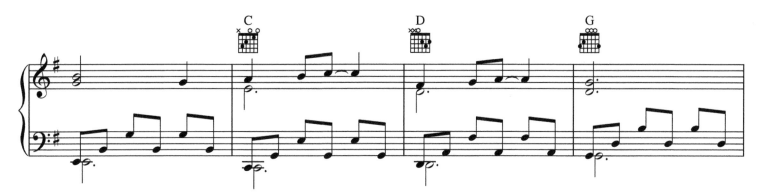

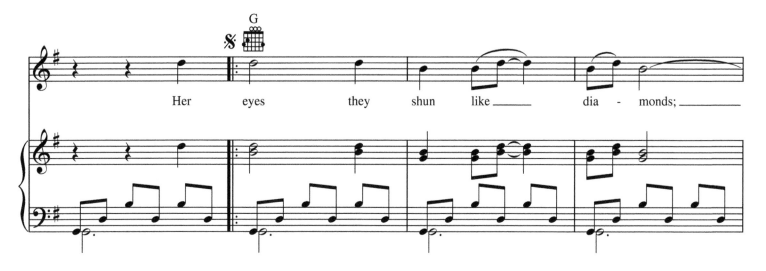

Her eyes they shun like ___ dia - monds; ___

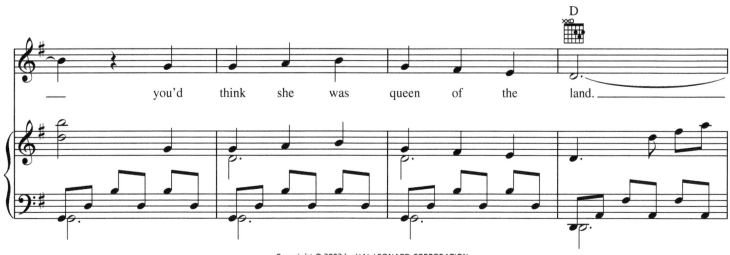

___ you'd think she was queen of the land. ___

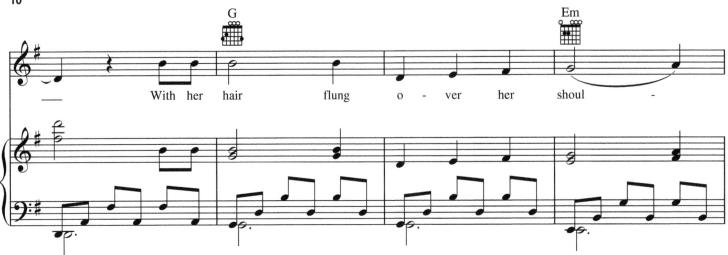

With her hair flung o - ver her shoul -

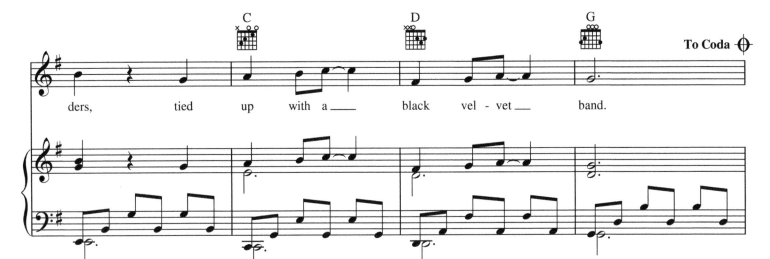

ders, tied up with a ___ black vel - vet ___ band.

To Coda ⊕

As I ___ went walk - ing down ___ Broad - way, ___
'Fore judge ___ and ju - ry next ___ morn - ing ___

___ not in - tend - ing to stay ver - y ___ long, ___
___ both of us did ___ ap - pear. ___

I met with this ___ frol- ick - some dam -
A gen - tle - man ___ claimed his ___ jew - el -

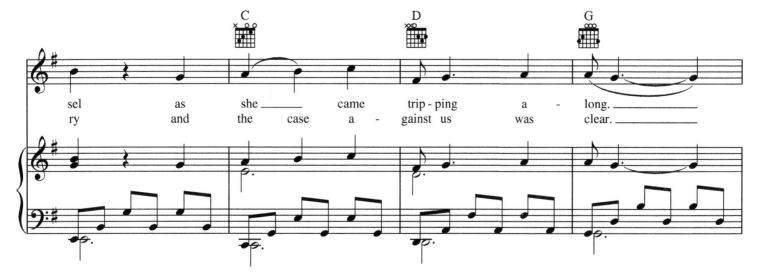

sel as she ___ came trip - ping a - long. ___
ry and the case a - gainst us was clear. ___

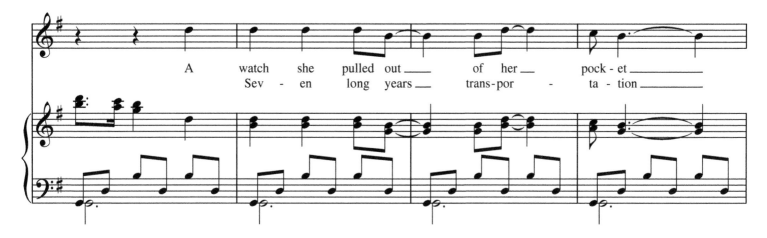

A watch she pulled out ___ of her ___ pock - et ___
Sev - en long years ___ trans - por - ta - tion ___

and slipped it right ___ in - to me ___ hand. ___
right on down to ___ Van Die - men's ___ Land; ___

On the ver - y first day that I ___ met ___
far a - way from my friends and com - pan -

her, bad luck to her ___ black vel - vet ___
ions to fol - low the ___ black vel - vet ___

band.   Her band.   Her

D.S. al Coda

CODA

Her eyes they shun like ___

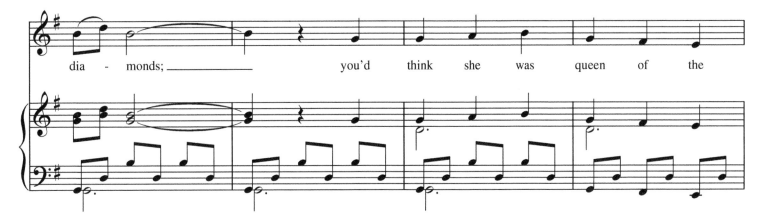

dia - monds; _____ you'd think she was queen of the

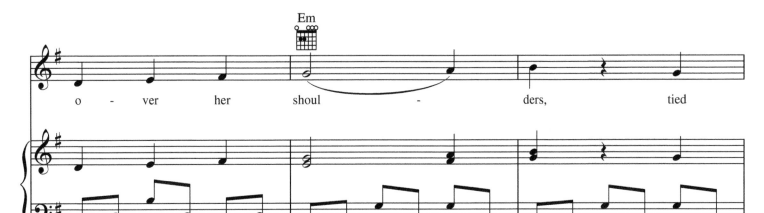

land. _____ With her hair flung

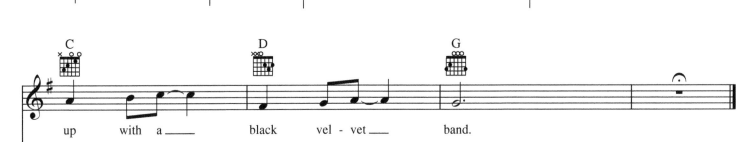

o - ver her shoul - ders, tied

up with a ___ black vel - vet ___ band.

BRENNAN ON THE MOOR

Traditional Irish Folk Song

Moderately

1. It's a-bout a fierce high-way-man my sto-ry I will
2. up-on the King's high-way Old Bren-nan he sat
3. Bren-nan's wife had gone to town pro-vi-sions for to
4.-6. *(See additional lyrics)*

tell. His name was Wil-ly Bren-nan and in Ire-land he did
down. He met the may-or of Moor-land five miles out-side of
buy, and when she saw her Wil-ly tak-en she be-gan to

dwell. 'Twas up-on the King's own moun-tain he be-gan his wild ca-reer, and
town. Now the may-or, he had heard of Bren-nan and, "I think," says he, "Your
cry. Says he, "Hand me that ten-pen-ny," and as soon as Wil-ly spoke, she

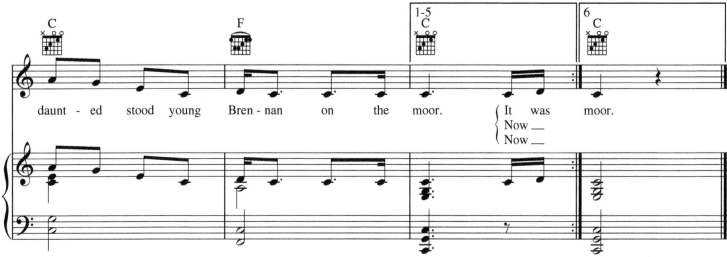

Additional Lyrics

4. Now Brennan got his blunderbuss, my story I'll unfold.
   He caused the mayor to tremble and deliver up his gold.
   Five thousand pounds were offered for his apprehension there,
   But Brennan and the peddler to the mountain did repair.
   Oh, it's Brennan on the moor, Brennan on the moor.
   Bold, gay and undaunted stood young Brennan on the moor.

5. Now Brennan is an outlaw all on some mountain high.
   With infantry and cavalry to take him they did try.
   But he laughed at them and he scorned at them until, it was said,
   By a false-hearted woman he was cruelly betrayed.
   Oh, it's Brennan on the moor, Brennan on the moor.
   Bold, gay and undaunted stood young Brennan on the moor.

6. They hung him at the crossroads; in chains he swung and died.
   But still they say that in the night some do see him ride.
   They see him with his blunderbuss in the midnight chill;
   Along, along the king's highway rides Willy Brennan still.
   Oh, it's Brennan on the moor, Brennan on the moor.
   Bold, gay and undaunted stood young Brennan on the moor.

A BUNCH OF THYME

Traditional Irish Folk Song

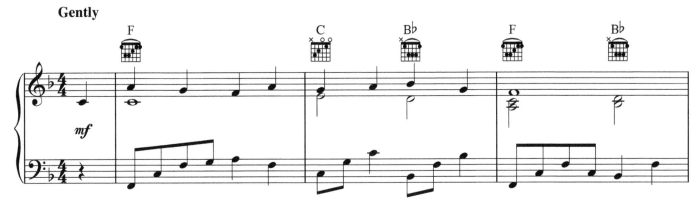

1.,5. Come all you mai - dens young and
thyme, it is a pre - cious
Once I had a bunch of
sail - or gave to me a

fair, all you that are bloom - ing in your
thing and thyme brings all things to my
thyme; I thought it nev - er would de -
rose, a rose that nev - er would de -

prime, _____ and al - ways be - ware _____ to
mind. _____ Thyme with all its fla - vors a -
cay. _____ Then came a lust - y sail - or who
cay. _____ He gave it to me _____ to

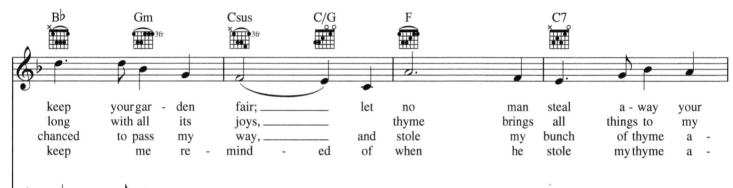

keep your gar - den fair; _____ let no man steal a - way your
long with all its joys, _____ let thyme brings all things to my
chanced to pass my way, _____ and stole my bunch of thyme a -
keep me re - mind - ed of when he stole my thyme a -

thyme. _____ For ___
mind. _____
way. _____ The
way. _____ Come

CLIFFS OF DONEEN

Traditional Irish Folk Song

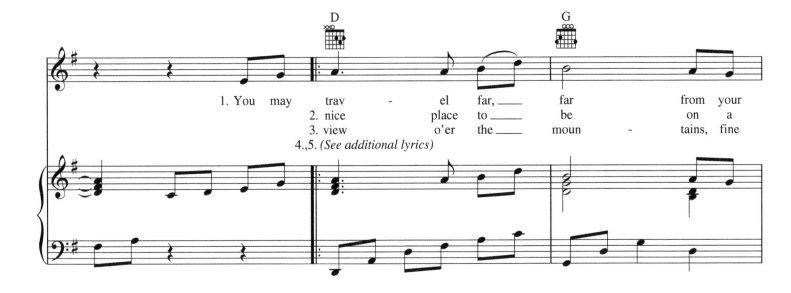

1. You may trav - el far, ____ far from your
2. nice place to ____ be on a
3. view o'er the ____ moun - tains, fine

4.,5. *(See additional lyrics)*

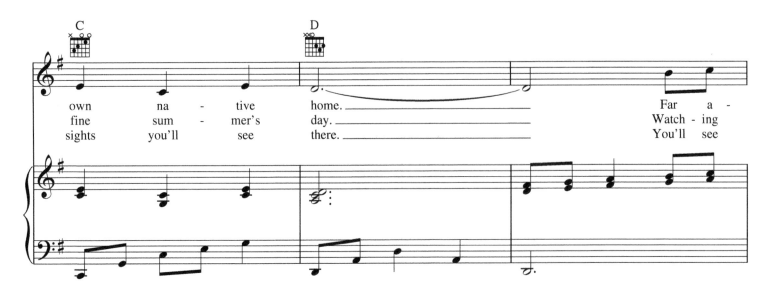

own na - tive home. ____ Far a -
fine sum - mer's day. ____ Watch - ing
sights you'll see there. ____ You'll see

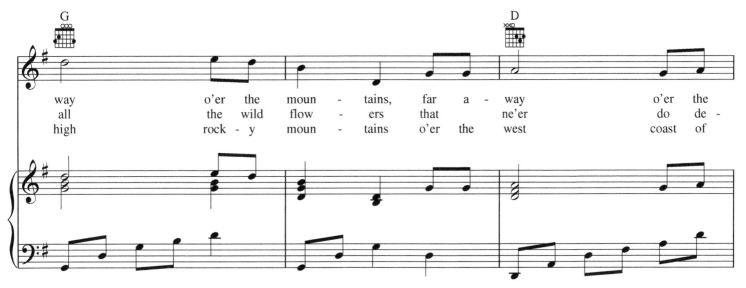

way .... o'er the moun - tains, far a - way .... o'er the
all .... the wild flow - ers that ne'er .... do de -
high .... rock - y moun - tains o'er the west .... coast of

foam. _____ But of all the fine
cay. _____ Oh, the hares and the
Clare. _____ Oh, the towns of Kil -

plac - es that I've ev - er been, _____
pheas - ants are plain to be seen, _____
kee and Kil - rush can be seen, _____

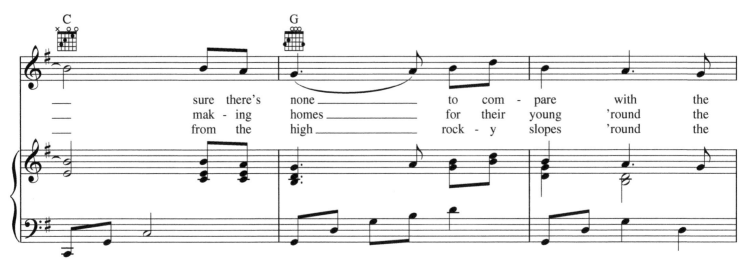

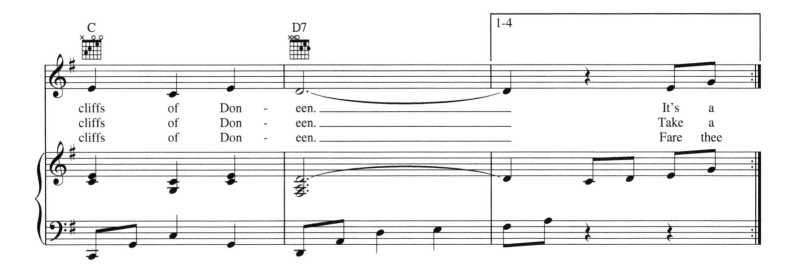

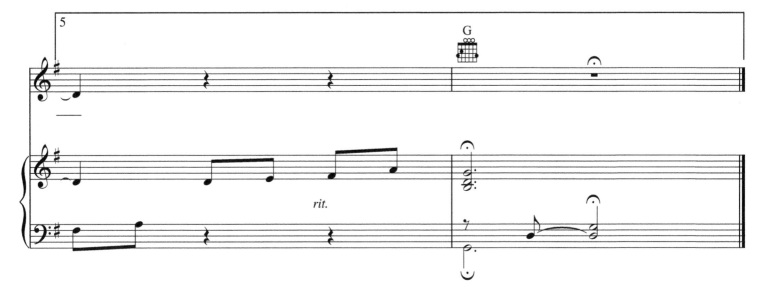

Additional Lyrics

4. Fare thee well to Doneen, fare thee well for a while
   And to all the kind people I'm leaving behind.
   To the streams and the meadows where late I have been,
   And the high rocky slopes 'round the cliffs of Doneen.

5. Fare thee well to Doneen, fare thee well for a while.
   And although we are parted by the raging sea wild,
   Once again I will walk with my Irish colleen
   'Round the high rocky slopes of the cliffs of Doneen.

FINNEGAN'S WAKE

Traditional Irish Folk Song

Moderately

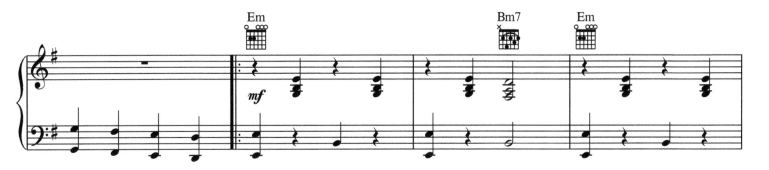

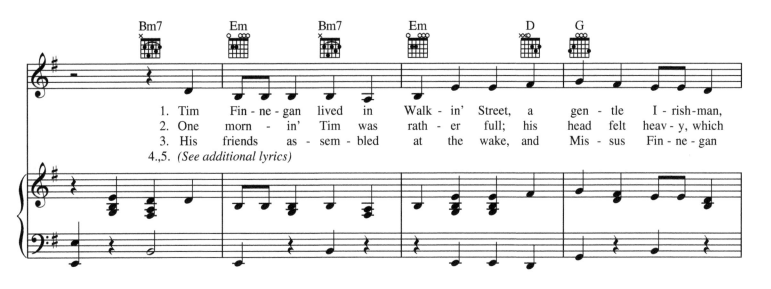

1. Tim Fin-ne-gan lived in Walk-in' Street, a gen-tle I-rish-man,
2. One morn-in' Tim was rath-er full; his head felt heav-y, which
3. His friends as-sem-bled at the wake, and Mis-sus Fin-ne-gan
4.,5. *(See additional lyrics)*

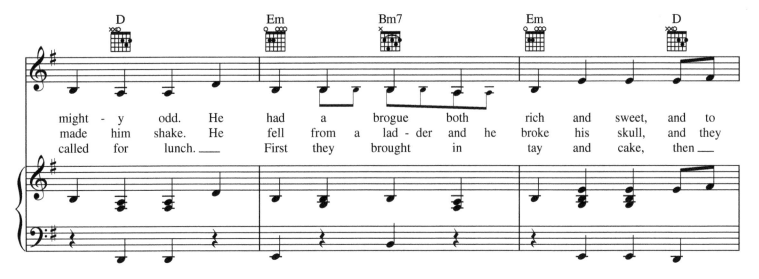

might-y odd. He had a brogue both rich and sweet, and to
made him shake. He fell from a lad-der and he broke his skull, and they
called for lunch. ___ First they brought in tay and cake, then ___

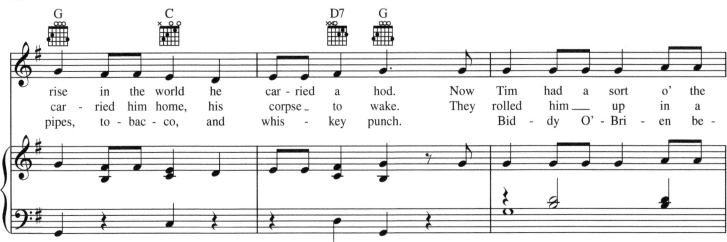

rise in the world he car - ried a hod.
Now Tim had a sort o' the
car - ried him home, his corpse _ to wake.
They rolled him ___ up in a
pipes, to - bac - co, and whis - key punch.
Bid - dy O' - Bri - en be -

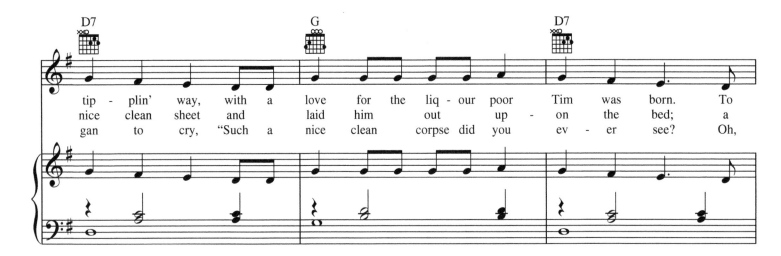

tip - plin' way, with a love for the liq - our poor Tim was born. To
nice clean sheet and laid him out up - on the bed; a
gan to cry, "Such a nice clean corpse did you ev - er see? Oh,

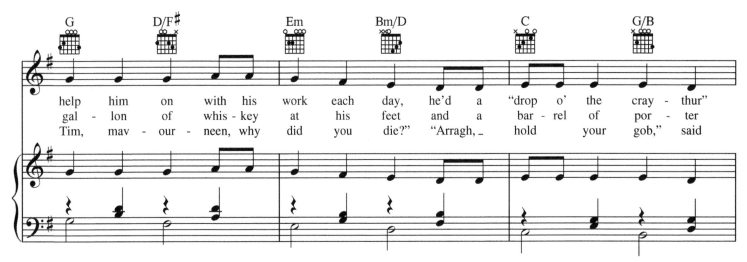

help him on with his work each day, he'd a "drop o' the cray - thur"
gal - lon of whis - key at his feet and a bar - rel of por - ter
Tim, mav - our - neen, why did you die?" "Arragh, _ hold your gob," said

Chorus

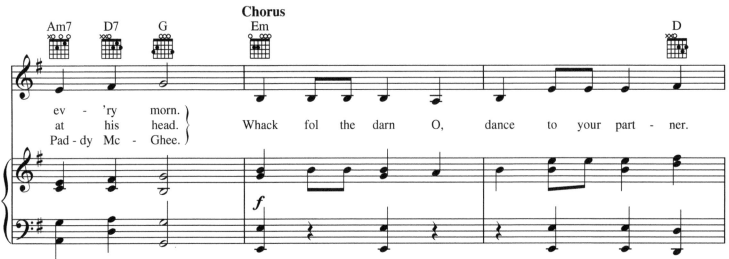

ev - 'ry morn.
at his head.
Pad - dy Mc - Ghee.
Whack fol the darn O, dance to your part - ner.

f

Additional Lyrics

4. Then Maggie O'Connor took up the job,
   "Oh Biddy," says she, "you're wrong, I'm sure."
   Biddy, she gave her a belt in the gob
   And left her sprawlin' on the floor.
   And then the war did soon engage,
   'Twas woman to woman and man to man.
   Shillelaigh law was all the rage,
   And a row and ruction soon began.
   Chorus

5. Then Mickey Maloney ducked his head
   When a noggin of whiskey flew at him.
   It missed, and falling on the bed,
   The liquor scattered over Tim!
   The corpse revives; see how he rises!
   Timothy, rising from the bed,
   Said, "Whirl your whiskey around like blazes,
   Thanum an Dhul! Do you think I'm dead?"
   Chorus

DANNY BOY
(Londonderry Air)

Words by FREDERICK EDWARD WEATHERLY
Traditional Irish Folk Melody

back when sum-mer's in the mead - ow, ___ or when the val - ley's hush'd and white with
hear, tho' soft your tread a - bove ___ me, ___ and all my dreams will warm and sweet - er

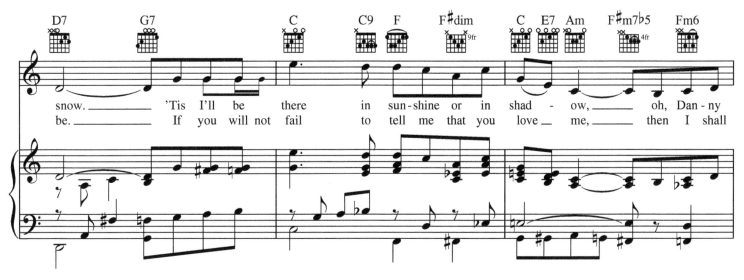

snow. _____ 'Tis I'll be there in sun - shine or in shad - ow, _____ oh, Dan - ny
be. _____ If you will not fail to tell me that you love ___ me, _____ then I shall

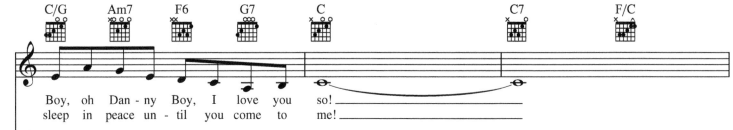

Boy, oh Dan - ny Boy, I love you so! _____
sleep in peace un - til you come to me! _____

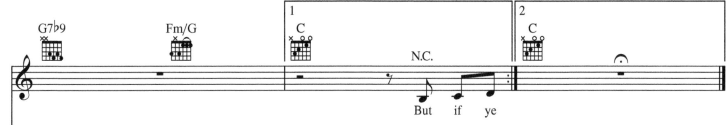

But if ye

DICEY REILLY

Traditional Irish Folk Song

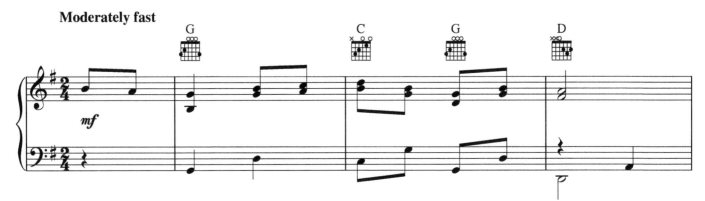

Moderately fast

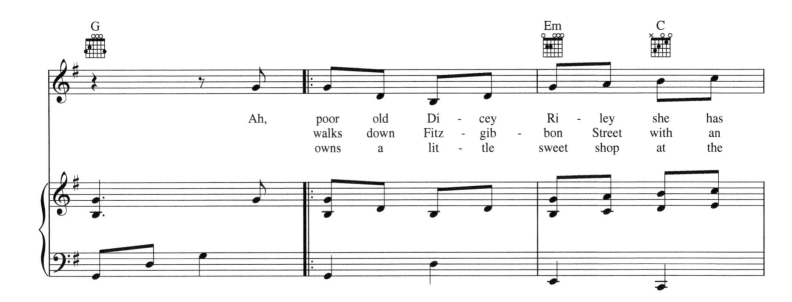

Ah, poor old Di - cey Ri - ley she has
walks down Fitz - gib - bon Street with an
owns a lit - tle sweet shop at the

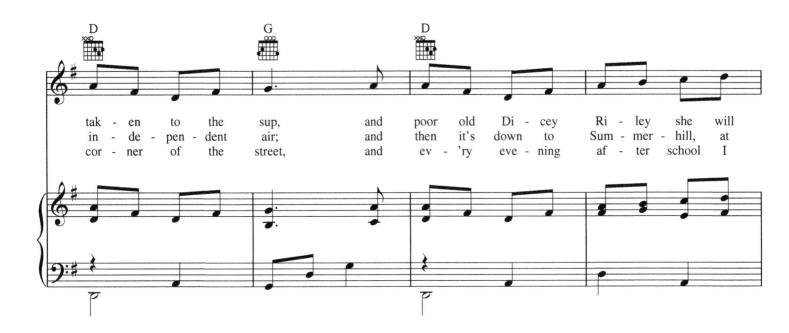

tak - en to the sup, and poor old Di - cey Ri - ley she will
in - de - pen - dent air; and then it's down to Sum - mer - hill, at
cor - ner of the street, and ev - 'ry eve - ning af - ter school I

never give it up, it's ___ off each morn - ing to the pop and ___
her the peo - ple stare. She ___ says, "It's near - ly half past one, so I'll
go to wash her feet. She ___ leaves me there to mind the shop, while she

then she's in for an - oth - er lit - tle drop.
nip ___ in for an - oth - er lit - tle one." } Ah, the heart of the rowl is Di - cey
nips ___ in for an - oth - er lit - tle drop.

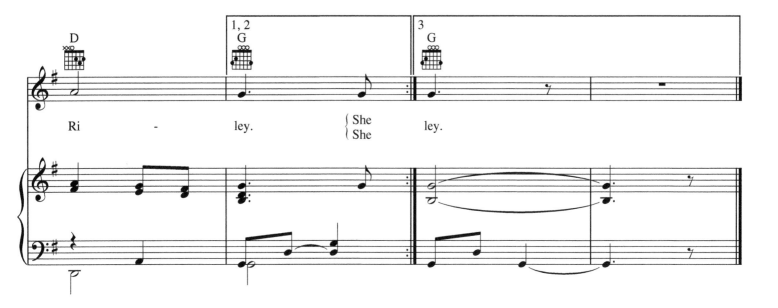

Ri - ley.
{ She
{ She ley.

DO YOU WANT YOUR OLD LOBBY

Traditional Irish Folk Song

Lively Waltz

I've a nice lit - tle cot and a small bit of
day the old land - lord came by for his
boys look so bash - ful when they go out

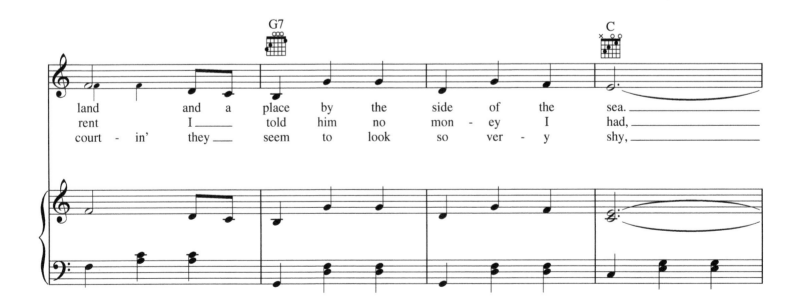

land and a place by the side of the sea. ____
rent I ____ told him no mon - ey I had, ____
court - in' they ____ seem to look so ver - y shy, ____

And I care a - bout no one, be - cause I be -
be - sides 'twas - n't fair ___ to ask me to
as to kiss a young maid, sure they seem half a -

lieve there's ___ no - bod - y cares a - bout me. ___
pay, the ___ times were so aw - ful - ly bad. ___
fraid, but they would if they could on the sly. ___

My peace is de - stroyed and I'm fair - ly an -
He felt dis - con - tent at not get - ting his
But me I do things in a dif - fer - ent

noyed, by a las - sie who works in the town. ___
rent, and he shook his big head in a frown, ___
way, I don't give a nod or a frown. ___

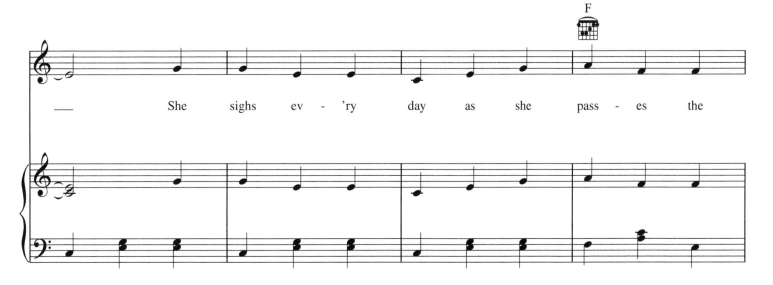

She sighs ev - 'ry day as she pass - es the

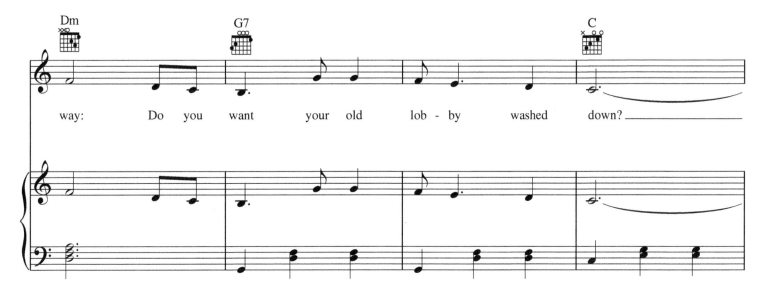

way: Do you want your old lob - by washed down? _____

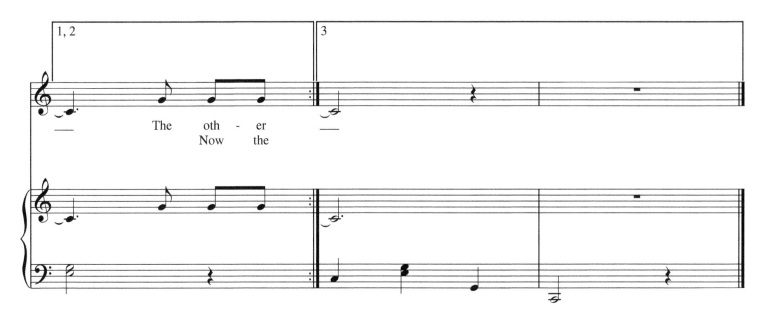

1, 2
The oth - er

3
Now the

THE FIELDS OF ATHENRY

Words and Music by
PETE ST. JOHN

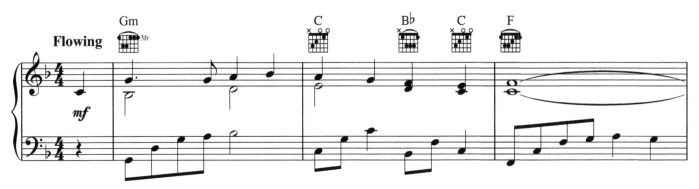

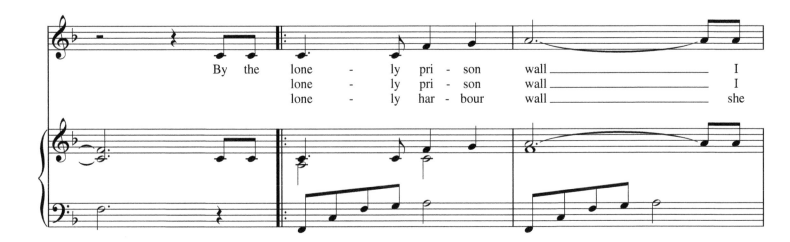

By the lone - ly pri - son wall _____ I
lone - ly pri - son wall _____ I
lone - ly har - bour wall _____ she

heard a young girl call - ing,
heard a young man call - ing,
watched the last star fall - ing,

Mi - chael, they are tak - ing you a -
noth - ing mat - ters Mar - y when you're
and that pri - son ship sailed out a - gainst the

way. _____
free. _____
sky. _____

For you stole Tre - vel - yn's
A - gainst the fa - mine and the
Sure she'll wait and hope and

corn so the young might see ___ the morn. Now a
Crown, I re - belled, they ran ___ me down, now
pray for her love in Bo - tan - y Bay, it's so

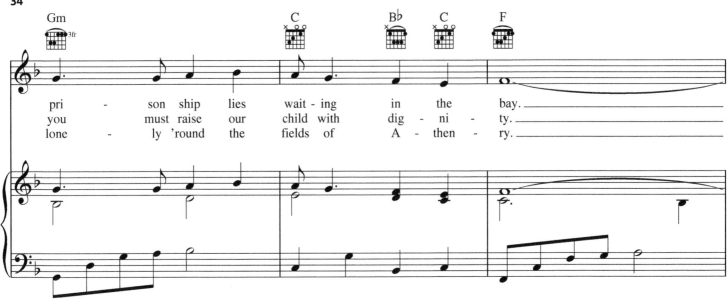

pri - son ship lies wait - ing in the bay.____
you must raise our child with dig - ni - ty.____
lone - ly 'round the fields of A - then - ry.____

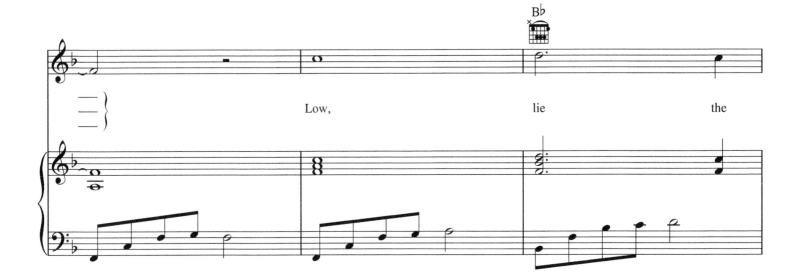

Low, lie the

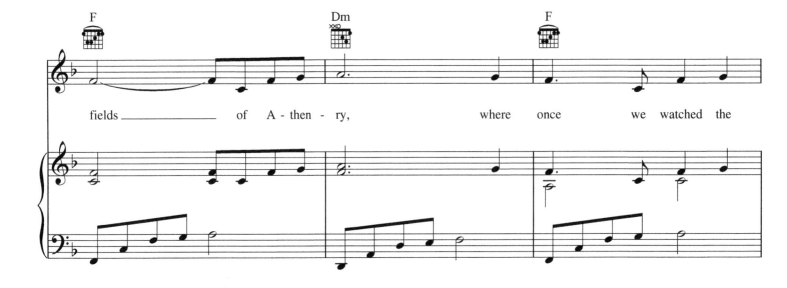

fields ____ of A - then - ry, where once we watched the

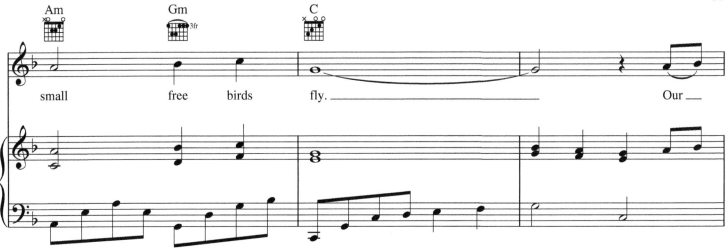

small   free   birds   fly._____   Our ___

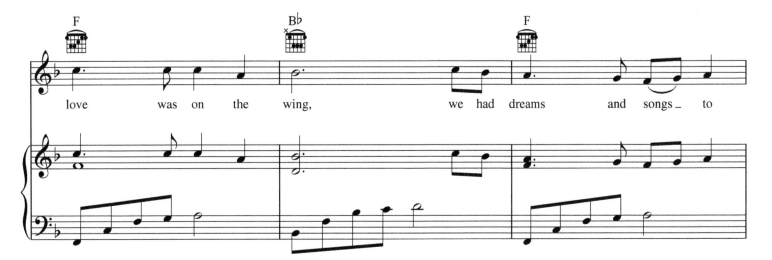

love   was   on   the   wing,   we had dreams   and songs _ to

sing.   It's   so   lone - ly 'round   the   fields   of   A - then -

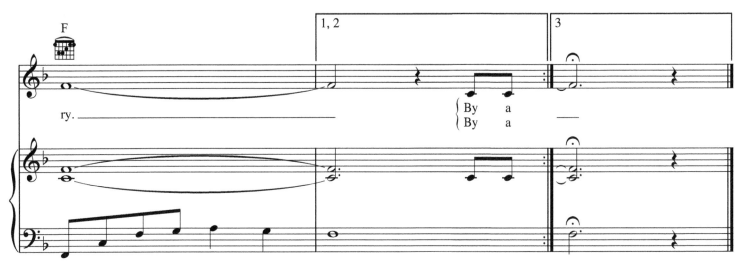

ry._____

1, 2

3

By   a
By   a

THE GERMAN CLOCKWINDER

Traditional Irish Folk Song

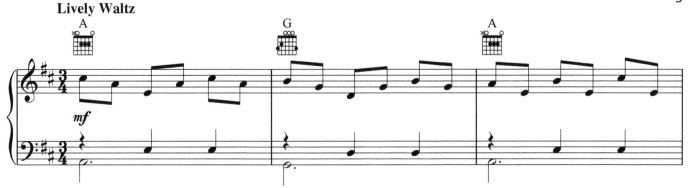

A Ger - man clock - wind - er to
was a young la - dy from
as they were seat - ed
hus - band says he, "Now look

Dub - lin once came, Ben - ja - min
Gros - ven - or Square, who said that her
down on the floor there came this
here Mar - y Anne, don't let that bold

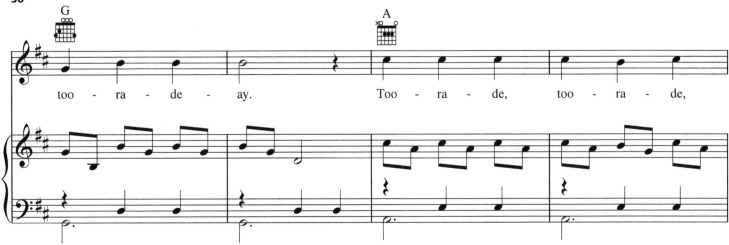

too - ra - de - ay. Too - ra - de, too - ra - de,

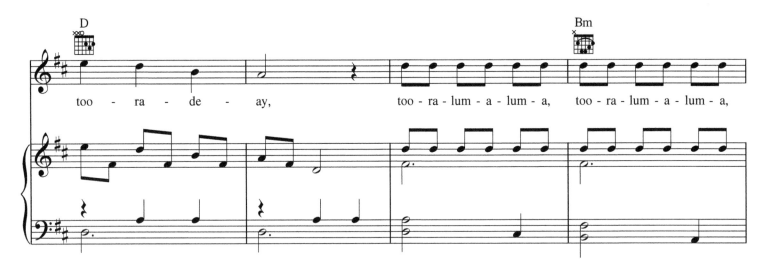

too - ra - de - ay, too - ra - lum - a - lum - a, too - ra - lum - a - lum - a,

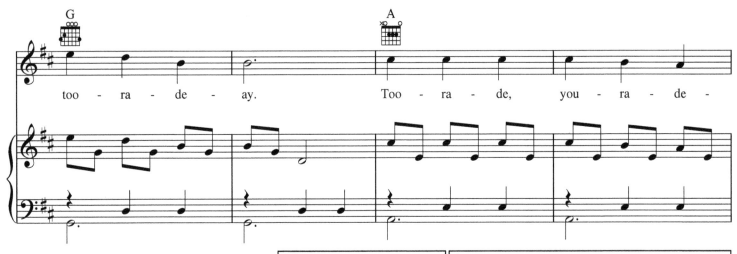

too - ra - de - ay. Too - ra - de, you - ra - de -

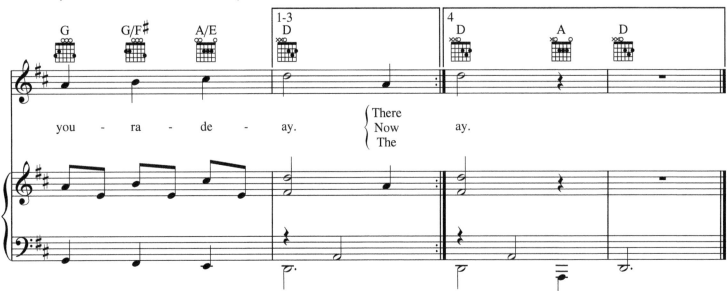

you - ra - de - ay. There Now ay. The

HILLS OF CONNEMARA

Spirited

Traditional Irish Folk Song

1. Gath - er up the pots and the old tin can, the mash, the corn, the bar - ley and the bran. Run like the dev - il from the ex - cise man keep the smoke from ri - sing, Bar - ney. Keep your ra.

2. eyes well peeled to - day, the tall, the tall men are on their way. Search - ing for the moun - tain tay, in the hills of Con - ne - ma - ra. Swing to the

3. left and swing to the right, the ex - cise men will dance all night. Drink - ing up the tay till the broad day - light, in the hills of Con - ne - ma - ra. A gal - lon for the

4., 5. (See additional lyrics)

Additional Lyrics

4. A gallon for the butcher, a quart for Tom,
   A bottle for poor old Father Tom,
   To help the poor old dear along,
   In the hills of Connemara.

5. Stand your ground, it is too late,
   The excise men are at the gate,
   Glory be to Paddy, but they're drinking it nate,
   In the hills of Connemara.

THE HUMOUR IS ON ME NOW

Traditional Irish Folk Song

1. As _____ I went out one morn-ing, it be-ing the month of
2. qui-et you fool-ish daugh-ter, and hold your sim-ple
3. who are you to turn me, that mar-ried young your-
4. deed I'll tell my moth-er the aw-ful things you
5.-8. *(See additional lyrics)*

May, a farm-er and his daugh-ter _____ I spied up-on my
tongue. You're bet-ter free and sin-gle, _____ and hap-py while you're
self, and took my dar-ling moth-er _____ from off the sin-gle
say, in-deed I'll tell my moth-er _____ this ver-y bless-ed

way. And the girl sat down quite calm-ly to the milk-ing of her
young. But the daugh-ter shook her shoul-ders and _____ milked her pat-ient
shelf? Ah sure, daugh-ter dear, so ais-y, and _____ milk your pa-tient
day. Och, now daugh-ter, have a heart, dear, you'll _____ start a fear-ful

Additional Lyrics

5. Och, if you must be married will you tell me who's the man?
   And quickly she did answer, "There's William, James and John,
   A carpenter, a tailor, and a man to milk the cow,
   For I will and I must get married and the humour is on me now."

6. A carpenter's a sharp man, and a tailor's hard to face,
   With his legs across the table and his threads about the place.
   And sure John's a fearful tyrant and never lacks a row,
   But I will and I must be married for the humour is on me now.

7. Well, if you must be married, wiil you tell me what you'll do?
   "Sure I will," the daughter answered, "just the same as you.
   I'll be mistress of my dairy and my butter and my cow."
   And your husband too, I'll venture, for the humour is on you now.

8. So at last the daughter married and married well-to-do,
   And loved her darling husband for a month, a year or two.
   But John was all a tyrant and she quickly rued her vow,
   Saying, "I'm sorry that I married for the humour is off me now."

I NEVER WILL MARRY

Traditional Folk Song

1. I nev-er will mar-ry,
day as I ram-bled
heard a poor maid-en
4.,5. *(See additional lyrics)*

ry, I'll be no man's wife.
bled down by the sea-shore,
en make a pit-i-ful cry.

I in-tend to stay sin-
the wind it did whis-
She sound-ed so lone-

Additional Lyrics

4. "My love's gone and left me, he's the one I adore.
   I never will see him, no never, no more."

5. "The shells in the ocean will be my deathbed,
   And the fish in the water swim over my head."

6. She plunged her fair body in the water so deep.
   And she closed her pretty blue eyes in the water to sleep.

I'M A ROVER AND SELDOM SOBER

Traditional Irish Folk Song

Lyrics:

I'm a rov-er and sel-dom so-ber, I'm a rov-er o' high de-gree. It's when I'm drink-ing I'm al-ways think-ing how to gain my love's com-pa-ny.

1. Though the night be as dark as
2. He step-pit up to her bed-room
3. She raised her heid on her snaw-white
4.-7. (See additional lyrics)

dun - geon, no' a star to be seen a - bove, I will be guid - ed with - out a
win - dow, kneel - in' gen - tly up - on a stone, he rap - pit at her bed - room
pil - low, wi' her arms ____ a - boot her breast; "Wha' is that at my bed - room

stum - ble in - to the airms o' my ain true love. I'm a love."
win - dow; "Dar - lin' dear, do you lie a - lone?"
win - dow, dis - turb - in' me at my lang night's rest?"

Additional Lyrics

4. "It's only me, your ain true lover;
   Open the door and let me in,
   For I hae come on a lang journey
   And I'm near drenched to the skin."

5. She opened the door wi' the greatest pleasure,
   She opened the door and she let him in;
   They baith shook hands and embraced each other,
   Until the mornin' they lay as one.

6. The cocks were crawin', the birds were whistlin',
   The burns they ran free abune the brae;
   "Remember, lass, I'm a ploughman laddie
   And the fairmer I must obey."

7. "Noo, my lass, I must gang and leave thee,
   And though the hills they are high above,
   I will climb them wi' greater pleasure
   Since I been in the airms o' my love."

THE IRISH ROVER

Traditional Irish Folk Song

Moderately

In the

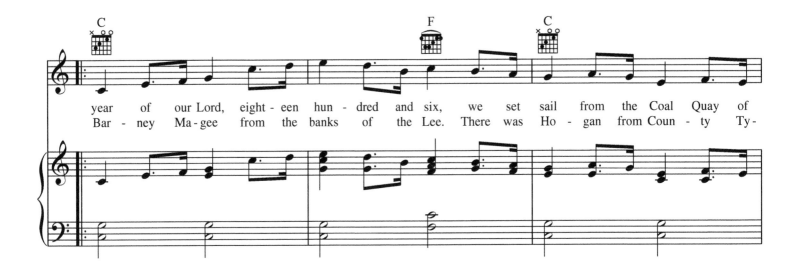

year of our Lord, eight-een hun-dred and six, we set sail from the Coal Quay of
Bar-ney Ma-gee from the banks of the Lee. There was Ho-gan from Coun-ty Ty-

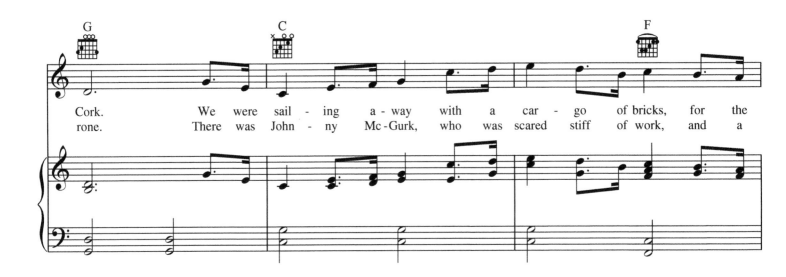

Cork. We were sail-ing a-way with a car-go of bricks, for the
rone. There was John-ny Mc-Gurk, who was scared stiff of work, and a

grand   cit - y   hall   in   New York.   We'd   an   el - e - gant craft,   it   was
chap   from   West-meath   named   Ma - lone.   There   was   Slug - ger   O' - Toole,   who   was

rigged   fore   and   aft,   and   how____   the   trade - winds   drove_____   her.   She   had
drunk   as   a   rule,   and   fight - ing   Bill   Tra - cy   from   Do - ver.   And   your

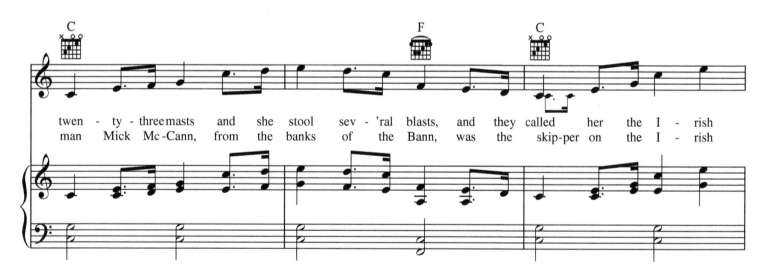

twen - ty - three masts   and   she   stool   sev - 'ral   blasts,   and   they   called   her   the   I - rish
man   Mick   Mc - Cann,   from   the   banks   of   the   Bann,   was   the   skip - per   on   the   I - rish

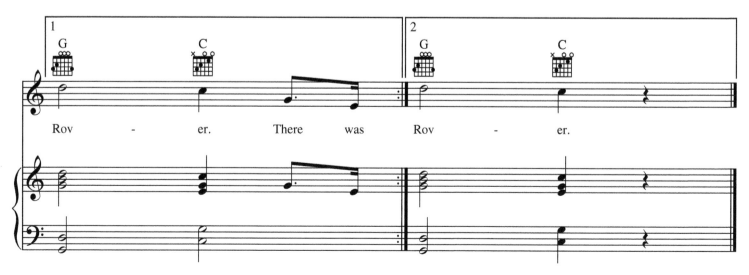

Rov - er.   There   was   Rov - er.

ISN'T IT GRAND, BOYS?

Traditional Irish Folk Song

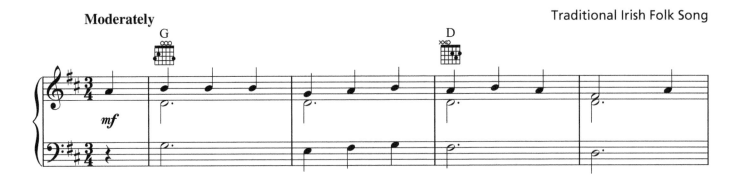

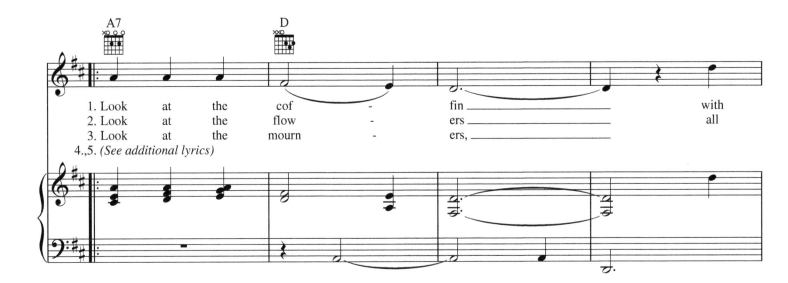

1. Look at the cof - fin _____ with
2. Look at the flow - ers _____ all
3. Look at the mourn - ers, _____
4.,5. *(See additional lyrics)*

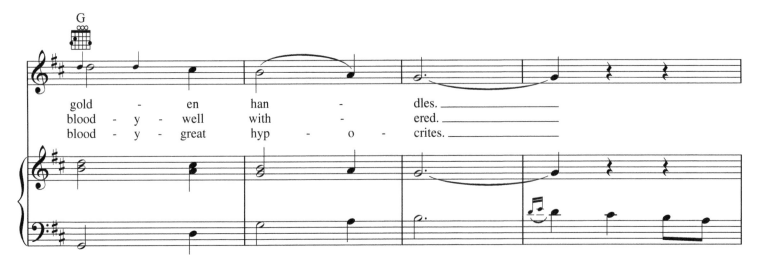

gold - en han - dles. _____
blood - y - well with - ered. _____
blood - y - great hyp - o - crites. _____

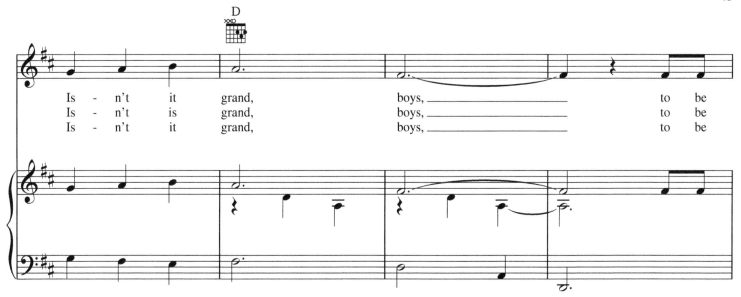

Is - n't it grand, boys, _____ to be
Is - n't is grand, boys, _____ to be
Is - n't it grand, boys, _____ to be

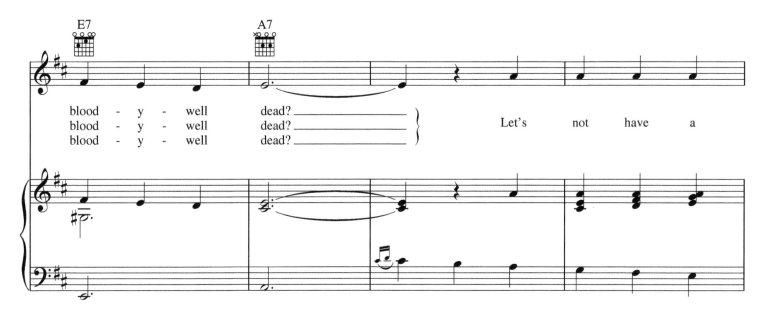

blood - y - well dead? _____
blood - y - well dead? _____   Let's not have a
blood - y - well dead? _____

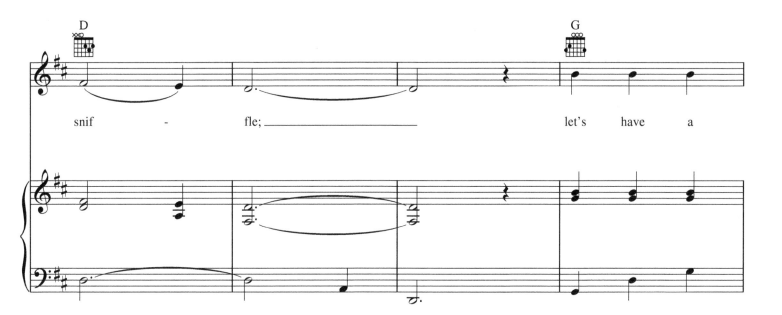

snif - fle; _____ let's have a

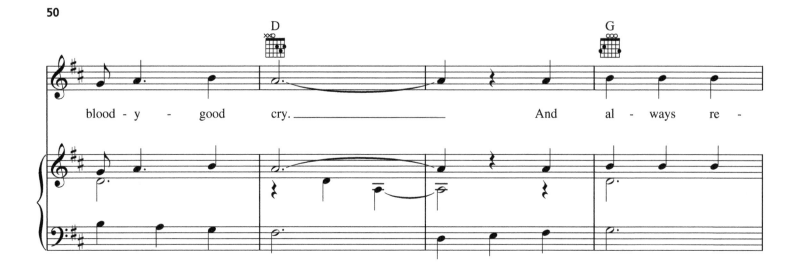

blood - y - good cry. _____ And al - ways re -

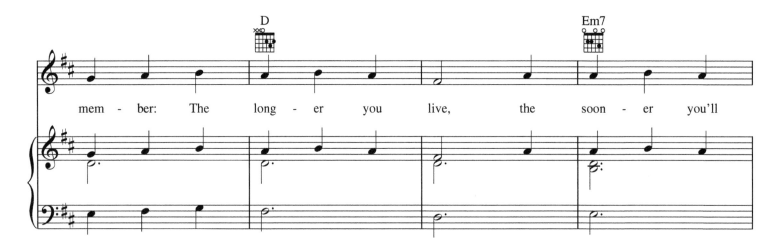

mem - ber: The long - er you live, the soon - er you'll

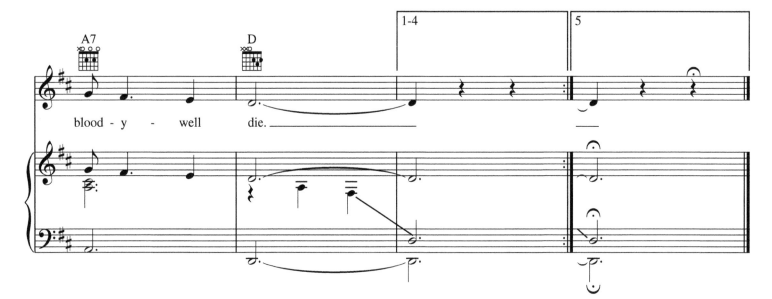

blood - y - well die. _____

Additional Lyrics

4. Look at the preacher,
   Bloody-nice fellow.
   Isn't it grand, boys,
   To be bloody-well dead?

5. Look at the widow,
   Bloody-great female.
   Isn't it grand, boys,
   It be bloody-well dead?

A NATION ONCE AGAIN

Words and Music by
THOMAS DAVIS

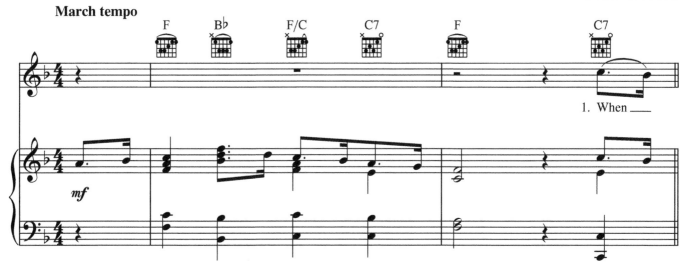

1. When ___

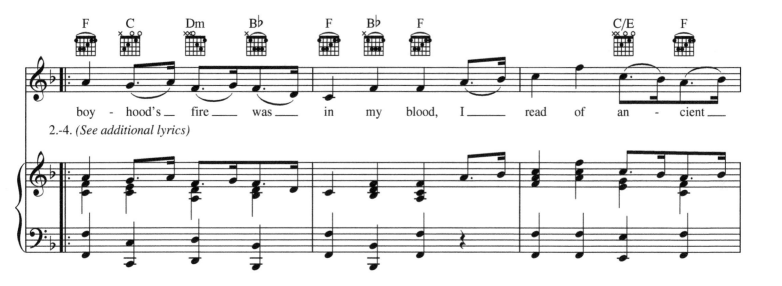

boy - hood's ___ fire ___ was ___ in my blood, I ___ read of an - cient ___
2.-4. (See additional lyrics)

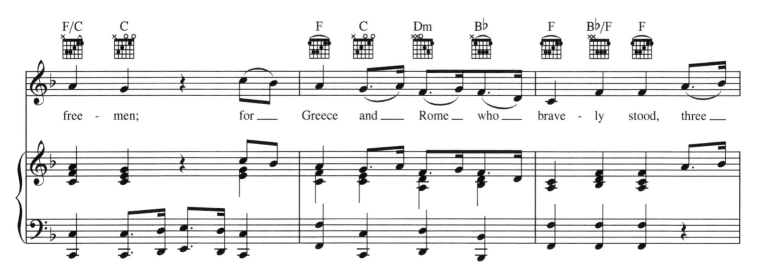

free - men; for ___ Greece and ___ Rome who ___ brave - ly stood, three ___

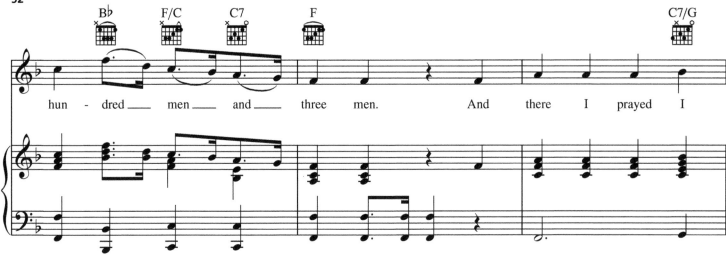

hun - dred ___ men ___ and ___ three men. And there I prayed I

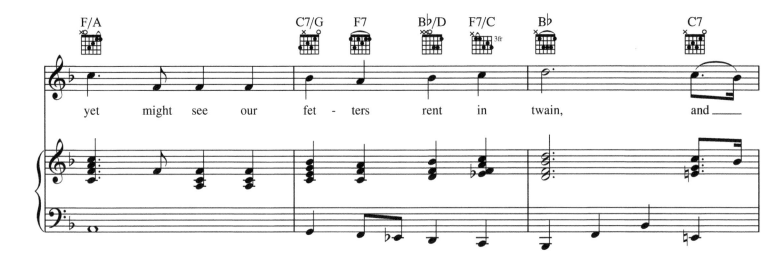

yet might see our fet - ters rent in twain, and ___

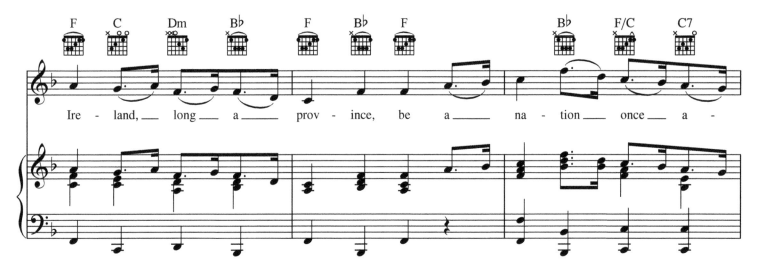

Ire - land, ___ long ___ a ___ prov - ince, be a ___ na - tion ___ once ___ a -

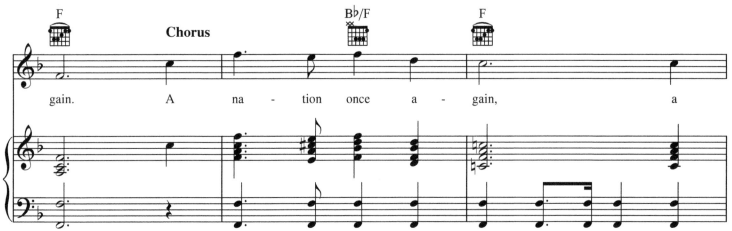

gain. A na - tion once a - gain, a

Additional Lyrics

2. And from that time, through wildest woe,
   That hope has shown a far light;
   Nor could love's brightest summer glow
   Outshine that solemn starlight.
   It seemed to watch above my head
   In forum, field and fane;
   Its angel voice sang 'round my bed,
   "A nation once again."
   Chorus

3. It whispered too, that "Freedom's Ark"
   And service high and holy,
   Would be profaned by feelings dark
   And passions vain or lowly;
   For freedom comes from God's right hand,
   And needs a Godly train,
   And righteous men must make our land
   A nation once again.
   Chorus

4. So as I grew from boy to man,
   I bent me at that bidding;
   My spirit of each selfish plan
   And cruel passion ridding.
   For thus I hoped some day to aid.
   Oh! Can such hope be vain
   When my dear country shall be made
   A nation once again?
   Chorus

JOHNSON'S MOTOR CAR

Traditional Irish Folk Song

1. 'Twas down by Bran - ni - gan's Cor - ner, one
2. Bar - ney dear, be of good cheer, I'll
3. Dr. John - son heard the news he
4-6. *(See additional lyrics)*

morn - ing I did stray. I met a fel - low reb - el, and
tell you what we'll do. The spe - cials they are plen - ti - ful, the
soon put on his shoes. He says this is an ur - gent case there

to me he did say, "We've or - ders from the
I. R. A. are few. We'll send a wire to
is no time to lose. He then put on his

Additional Lyrics

4. But when he got to the railway bridge, some rebels he saw there.
   Old Johnson knew the game was up, for at him they did stare.
   He said, "I have a permit, to travel near and far."
   "To hell with your English permit, we want your motor car."

5. "What will my loyal brethren think, when they hear the news,
   My car it has been commandeered, by the rebels at Dunluce."
   "We'll give you a receipt for it, all signed by Captain Barr.
   And when Ireland gets her freedom, boy, you'll get your motor car."

6. Well, we put that car in motion and filled it to the brim,
   With guns and bayonets shining which made old Johnson grim,
   And Barney hoisted a Sinn Fein flag, and it fluttered like a star,
   And we gave three cheers for the I.R.A. and Johnson's motor car.

JUG OF PUNCH

Ulster Folk Song

'Twas ver - y

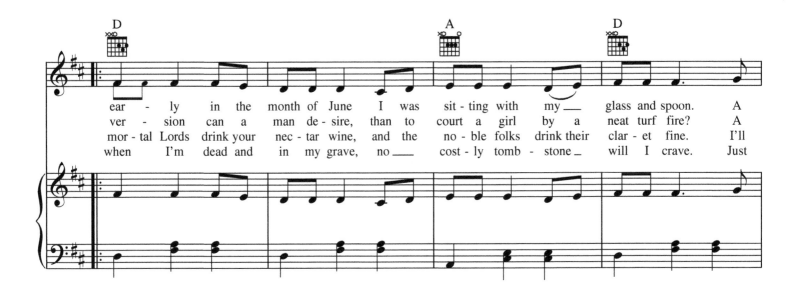

ear - ly in the month of June I was sit - ting with my __ glass and spoon. A
ver - sion can a man de - sire, than to court a girl by a neat turf fire? A
mor - tal Lords drink your nec - tar wine, and the no - ble folks drink their clar - et fine. I'll
when I'm dead and in my grave, no __ cost - ly tomb - stone __ will I crave. Just

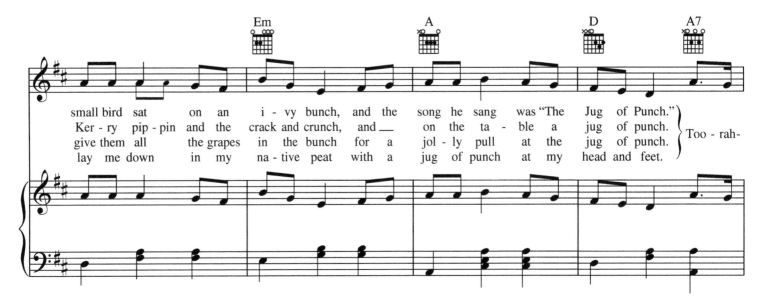

small bird sat on an i - vy bunch, and the song he sang was "The Jug of Punch."
Ker - ry pip - pin and the crack and crunch, and __ on the ta - ble a jug of punch.
give them all the grapes in the bunch for a jol - ly pull at the jug of punch.
lay me down in my na - tive peat with a jug of punch at my head and feet. } Too - rah-

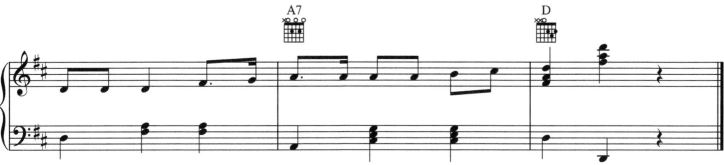

THE JUICE OF THE BARLEY

Traditional Irish Folk Song

1. In the sweet Coun - ty Lim - erick one cold win - ter's
2. I was a gas - soon of eight years or
3. learn - ing I wasn't such a gen - ius I'm
4.-6. *(See additional lyrics)*

night, all the turf fires were burn - ing when I saw the
so, with me turf and me pri - mer to school I did
think - ing but I soon bet the mas - ter en - tirely at drink -

light, and a drunk - en old mid - wife was tip - sy with
go, to a dust - y old school - house with - out an - y
ing, not a wake nor a wed - ding for five miles a -

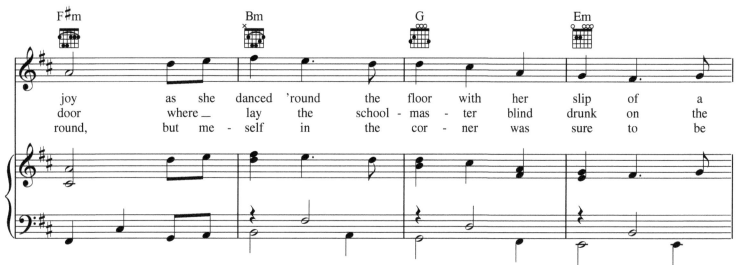

Chorus

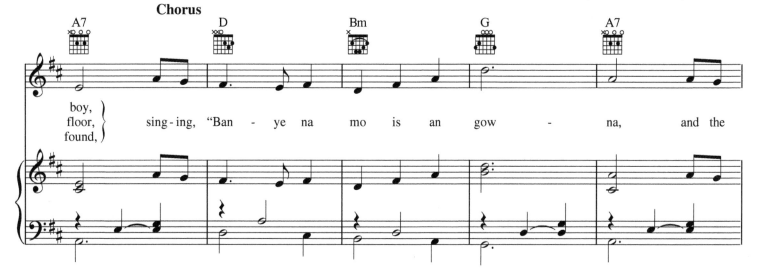

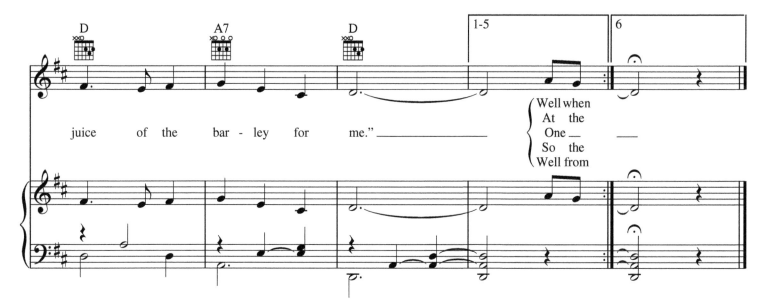

Additional Lyrics

4. One Sunday the priest read me out from the altar
   Saying, "You'll end up your days with your neck in a halter.
   And you'll dance a fine jig betwixt heaven and hell."
   And the words they did frighten, the truth for to tell.
   Chorus

5. So the very next morning as the dawn it did break,
   I went down to the vestry the pledge for to take
   And there in that room sat the priests in a bunch
   'Round a big roaring fire drinking tumblers of punch.
   Chorus

6. Well from that day to this I have wandered alone
   I'm a Jack of all Trades and a master of none.
   With the sky for me roof and the earth for me floor
   And I'll dance out me days drinking whiskey galore.
   Chorus

LEAVING OF LIVERPOOL

Irish Sea Chantey

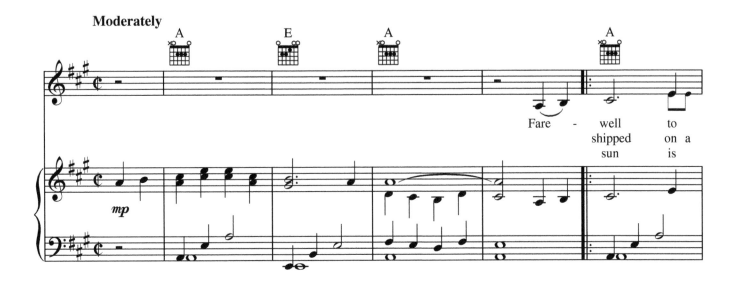

Fare - well to
shipped on a
sun is

you, __ my __ own true __ love; I am go - ing far a - way. ____
Yan - kee sail - ing __ ship; Da - vy Crock - ett is her __ name.
on __ the __ har - bour, __ love, and I wish I could re - main, ____

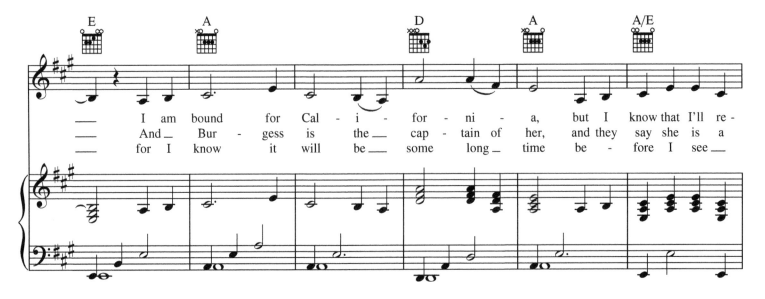

__ I am bound for Cal - i - for - ni - a, but I know that I'll re -
__ And __ Bur - gess is the __ cap - tain of her, and they say she is a
__ for I know it will be __ some long __ time be - fore I see __

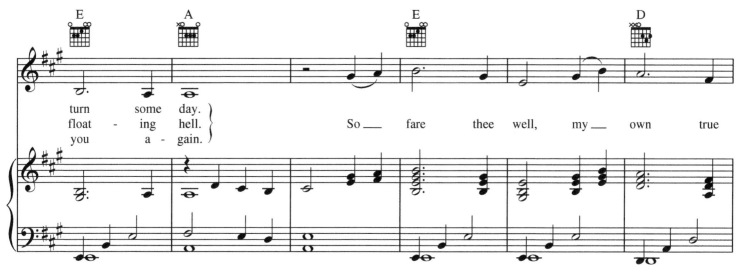

turn some day.
float - ing hell.
you a - gain.

So __ fare thee well, my __ own true

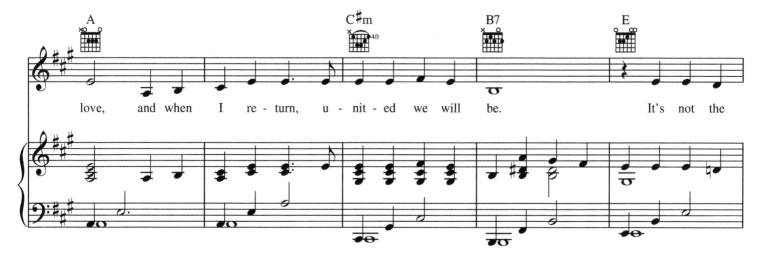

love, and when I re - turn, u - nit - ed we will be. It's not the

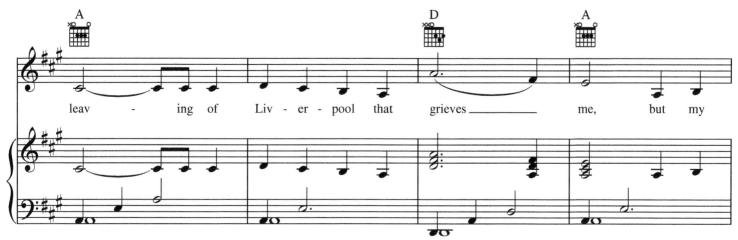

leav - ing of Liv - er - pool that grieves _____ me, but my

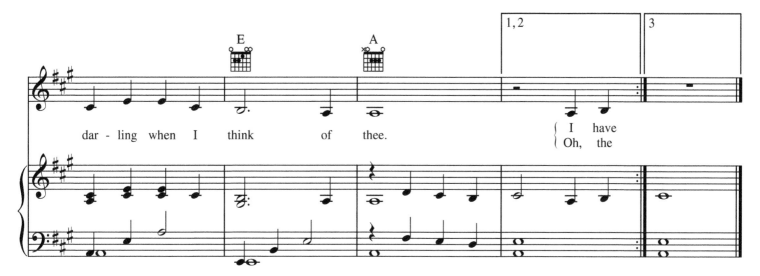

dar - ling when I think of thee.

I have
Oh, the

MacNAMARA'S BAND

Words by JOHN J. STAMFORD
Music by SHAMUS O'CONNOR

Saul. { band." } Oh! The drums go bang, and the cym - bals clang and the horns they blaze a -

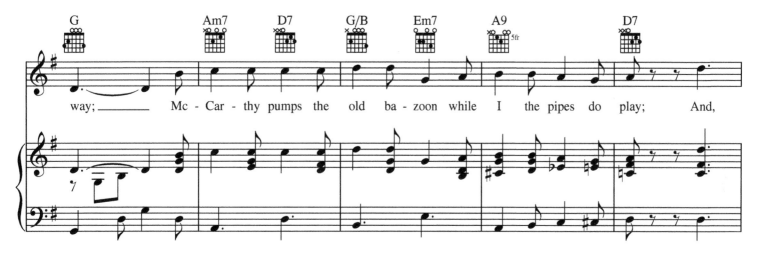

way; _____ Mc - Car - thy pumps the old ba - zoon while I the pipes do play; And,

Hen - nes - sey Ten - nes - see toot - les the flute, and the mu - sic is some - thing grand; _____ A

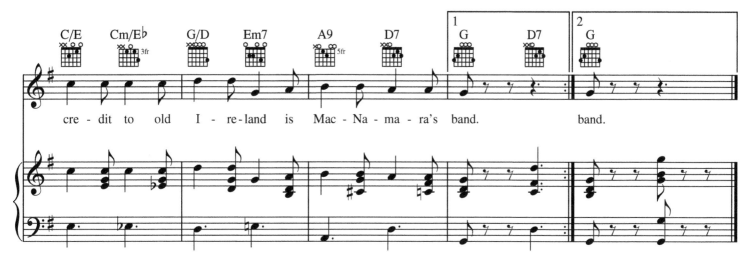

cre - dit to old I - re - land is Mac - Na - ma - ra's band. band.

MUIRSHEEN DURKIN

Traditional Irish Folk Song

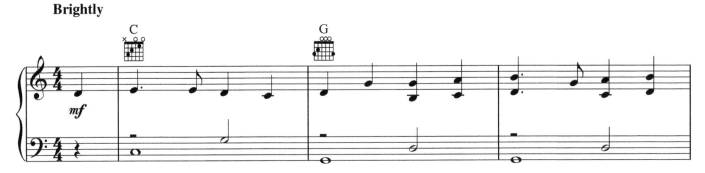

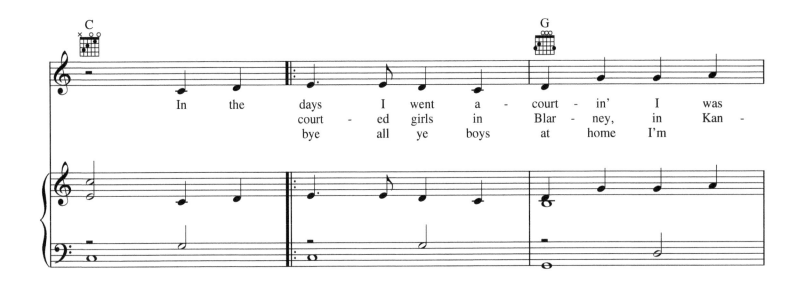

In the days I went a - court - in' I was
court - ed girls in Blar - ney, in Kan -
bye all ye boys at home I'm

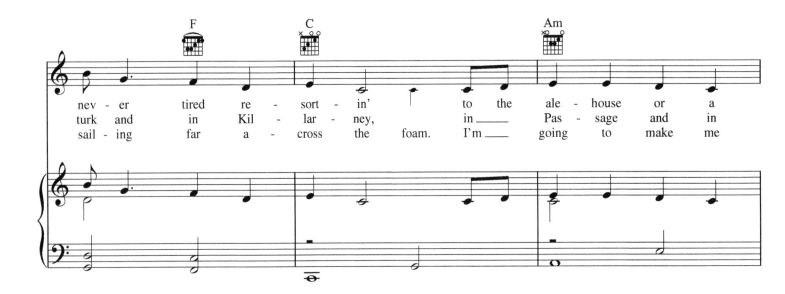

nev - er tired re - sort - in' to the ale - house or a
turk and in Kil - lar - ney, in Pas - sage and in
sail - ing far a - cross the foam. I'm going to make me

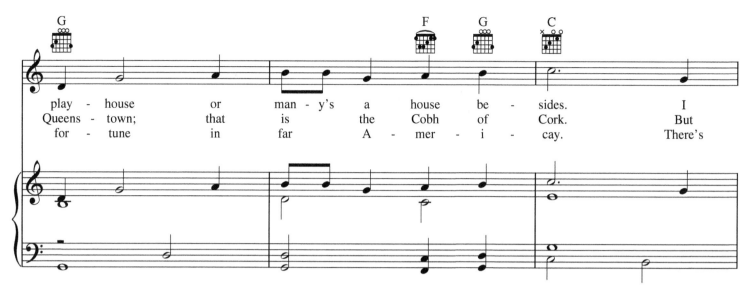

play - house — or man - y's a house be - sides. — I
Queens - town; that is the Cobh of Cork. — But
for - tune in far A - mer - i - cay. There's

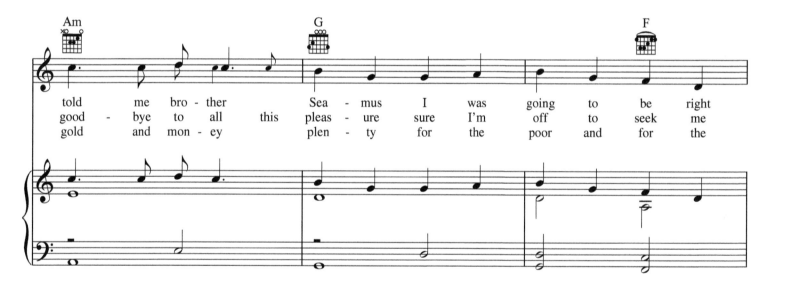

told me bro - ther Sea - mus I was going to be right
good - bye to all this pleas - ure sure I'm off to seek me
gold and mon - ey plen - ty for the poor and for the

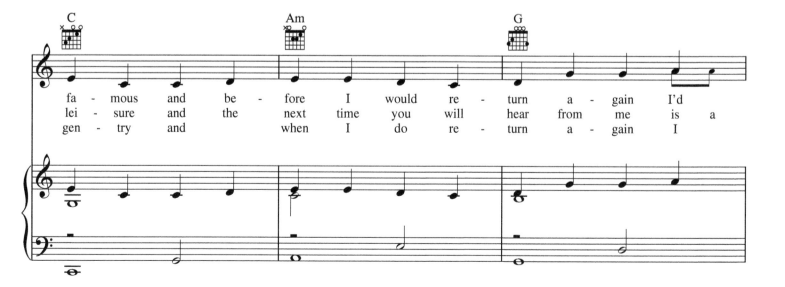

fa - mous and be - fore I would re - turn a - gain I'd
lei - sure and the next time you will hear from me is a
gen - try and when I do re - turn a - gain I

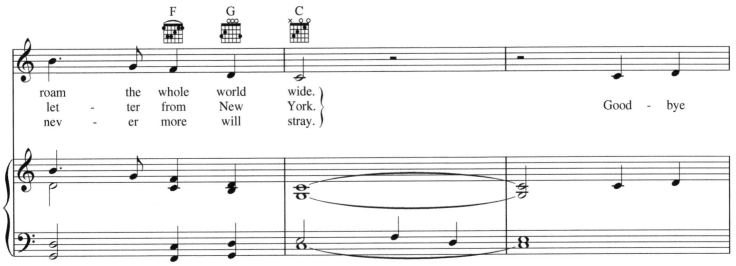

roam   the whole world wide.)
let - ter from New York.)
nev - er more will stray.)

Good - bye

Muir - sheen Dur - kin, sure I'm sick and tir - ed of _____

work in,' no _____ more I'll dig the pra - ties no

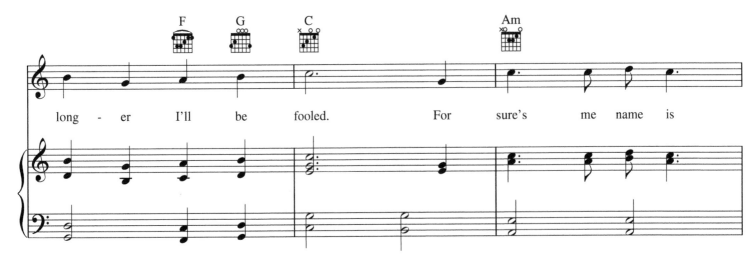

long - er I'll be fooled. For sure's me name is

Car - ney, I'll be off to Cal - i - for - nee and in -

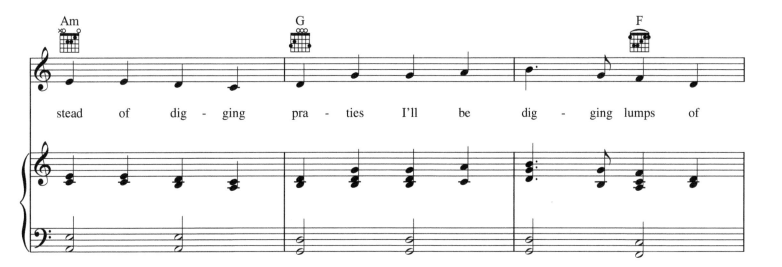

stead of dig - ging pra - ties I'll be dig - ging lumps of

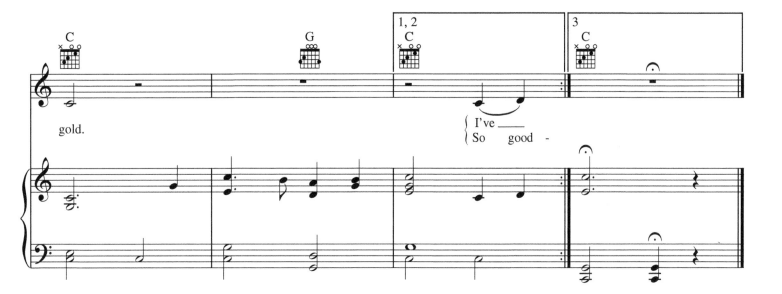

gold.

1, 2
I've ____

3
So good -

NORA

Traditional Irish Folk Song

The vio - lets were scent - ing the
gold - en robed daf - fo - dils

woods, Nor - a, dis - play - ing their
shone, Nor - a, and danced in the

charm to the bee, When I
breeze on the lea,

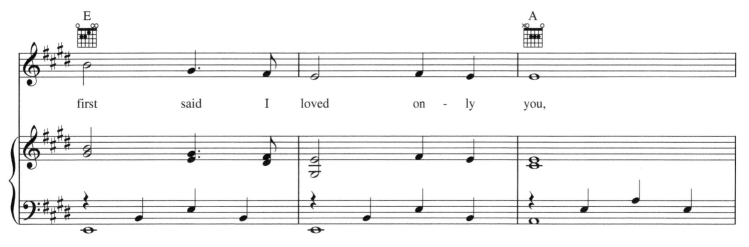

first said I loved on-ly you,

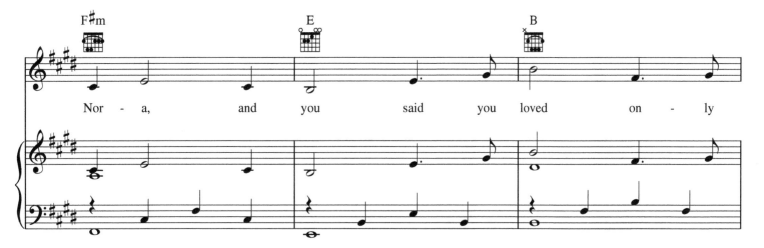

Nor - a, and you said you loved on - ly

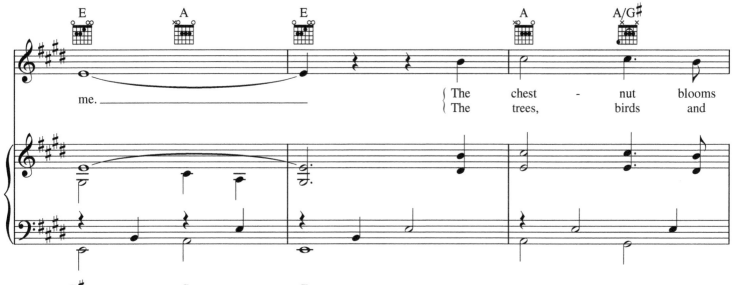

me. _____

The chest - nut blooms
The trees, birds and

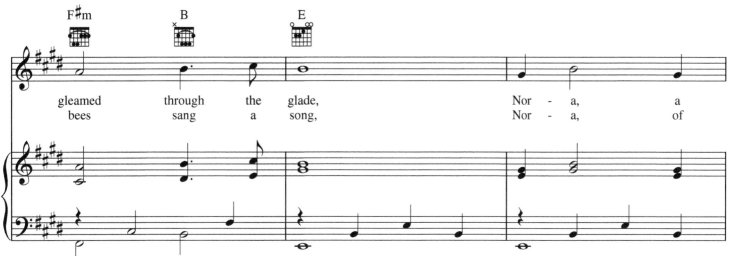

gleamed through the glade,
bees sang a song,

Nor - a, a
Nor - a, of

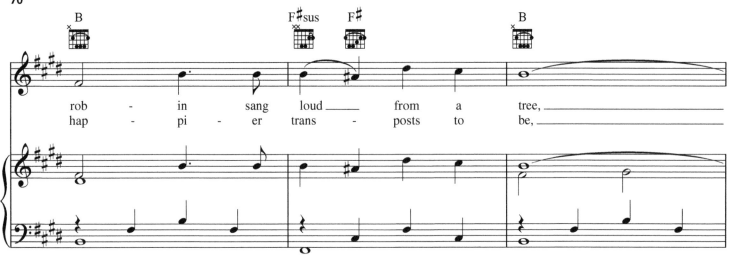

rob - in sang loud_____ from a tree,_____
hap - pi - er trans - posts to be,_____

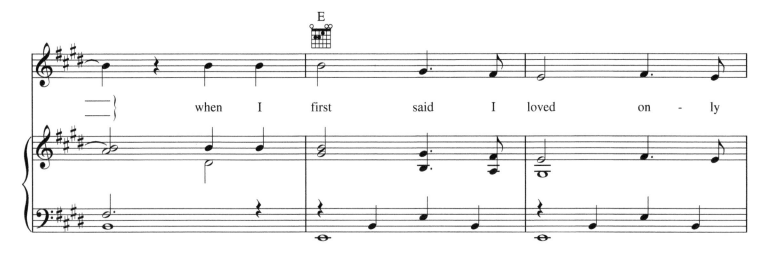

when I first said I loved on - ly

you, Nor - a, and you said you

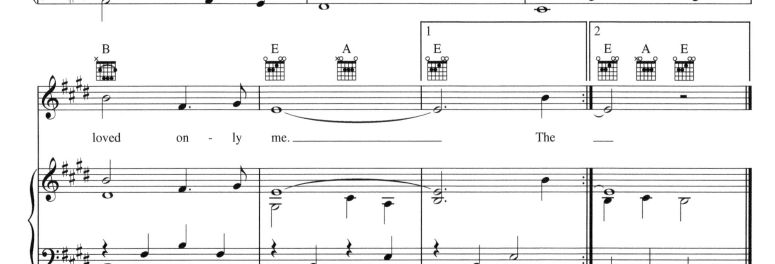

loved on - ly me._____ The_____

QUARE BUNGLE RYE

Traditional Irish Folk Song

Gently

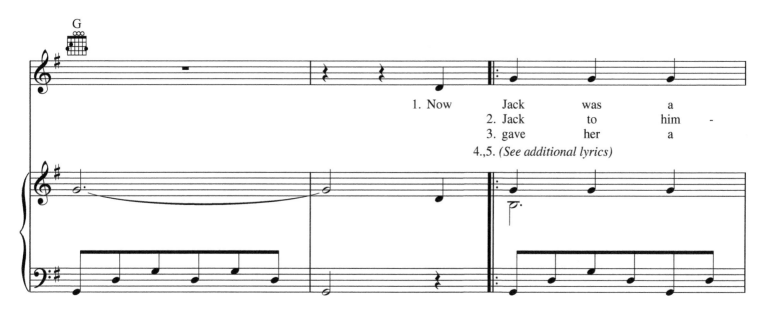

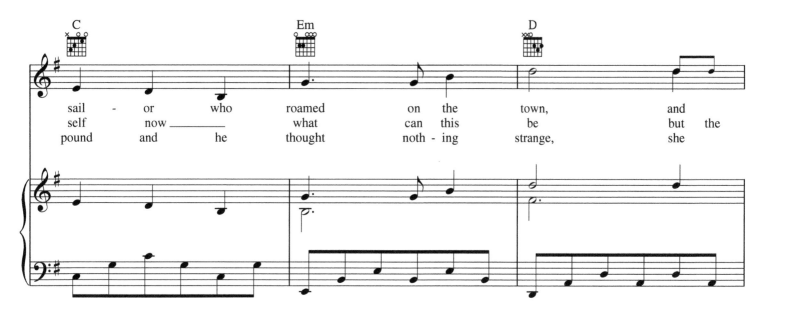

1. Now Jack was a
2. Jack to him -
3. gave her a
4.,5. *(See additional lyrics)*

sail - or who roamed on the town, and
self now _____ what can this be
pound and he thought noth - ing strange, but the

she was a dam - sel who skipped up and
fin - est of whis - key from old Ger - ma -
said, "Hold of that bas - ket till I run for your

down. Said the dam - sel to Jack and she
ny, smug - gled up sel in a bas - ket she and
change." Jack___ looked in the bas - ket and a

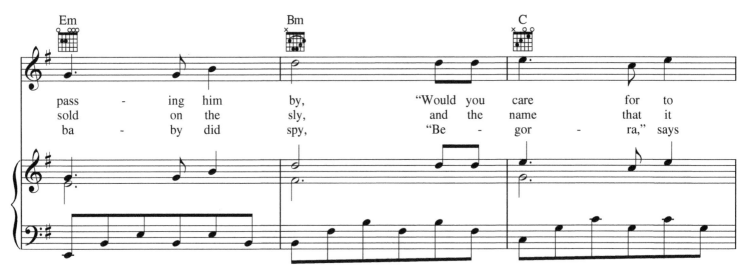

pass - ing him by, "Would you care for to
sold on the sly, and the name that it
ba - by did spy, "Be - gor - ra," says

pur - chase some quare bun - gle rye, rod - dy
goes by is quare bun - gle rye, rod - dy
he, "This is quare bun - gle rye, rod - dy

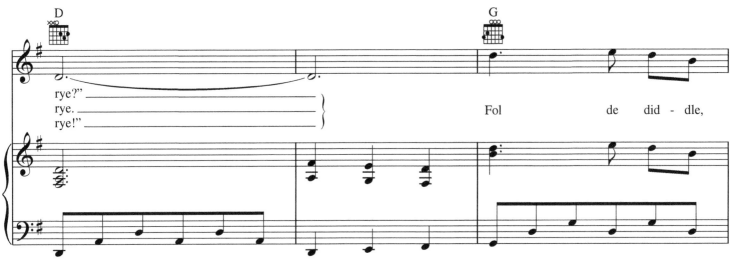

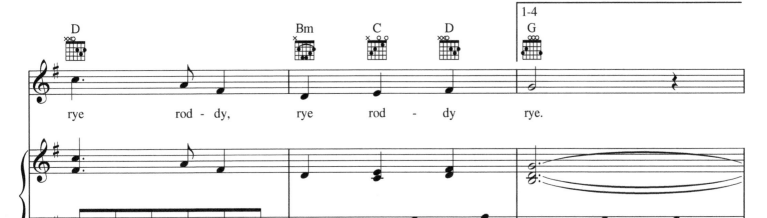

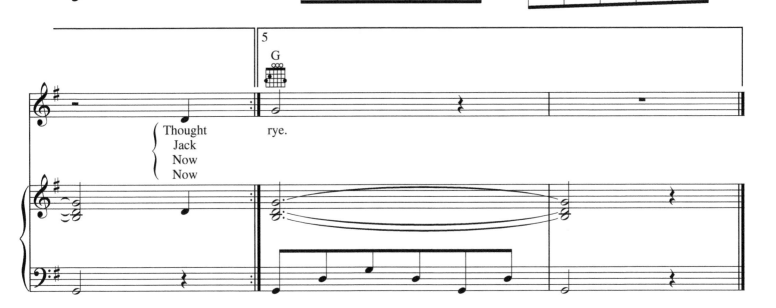

Additional Lyrics

4. Now to get the child christened was Jack's first intent
   And to get the child christened to the parson he went.
   Said the parson to Jack, "What will he go by?"
   "Bedad now," says Jack, "Call him quare bungle rye roddy rye."
   Fol de diddle, rye roddy, rye roddy rye.

5. Now all you bold sailors who roam on the town
   Beware of the damsels who skip up and down.
   Take a look in their baskets as they pass you by,
   Or else they may sell you some quare bungle rye roddy rye.
   Fol de diddle, rye roddy, rye roddy rye.

THE PARTING GLASS

Irish Folk Song

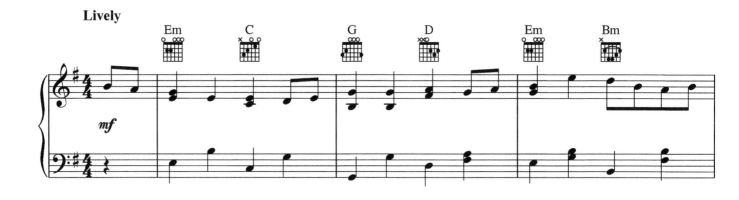

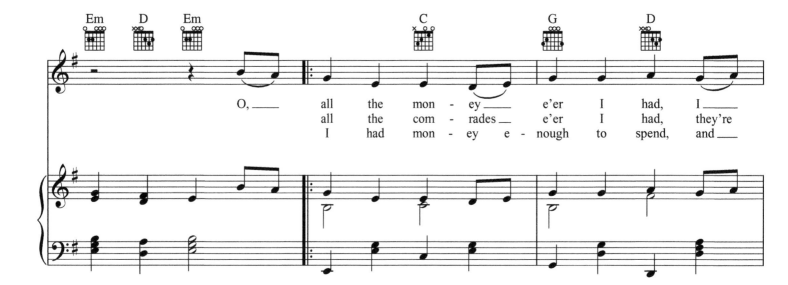

O, ___ all the mon - ey ___ e'er I had, I ___
all the com - rades ___ e'er I had, they're
I had mon - ey e - nough to spend, and ___

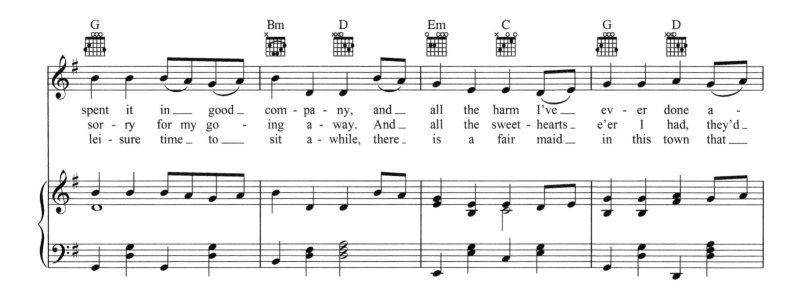

spent it in ___ good ___ com - pa - ny, and ___ all the harm I've ___ ev - er done a -
sor - ry for my go - ing a - way. And ___ all the sweet - hearts ___ e'er I had, they'd ___
lei - sure time ___ to ___ sit a - while, there ___ is a fair maid ___ in this town that ___

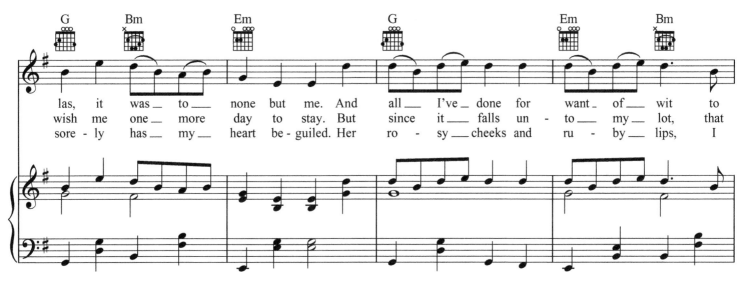

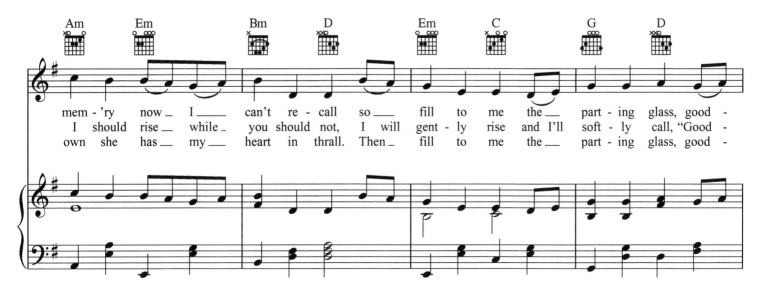

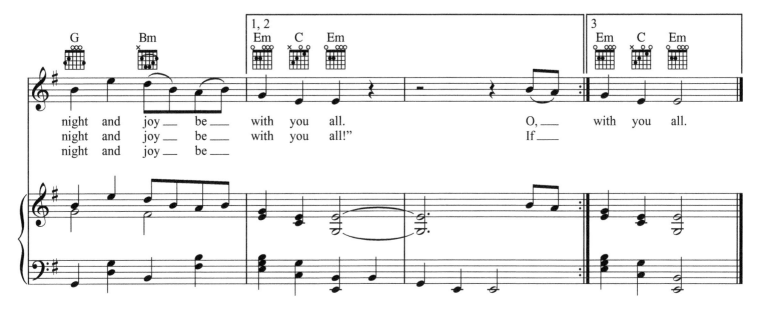

THE RARE OULD TIMES

Traditional Irish Folk Song

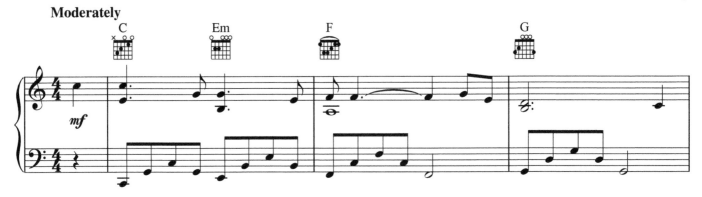

Moderately

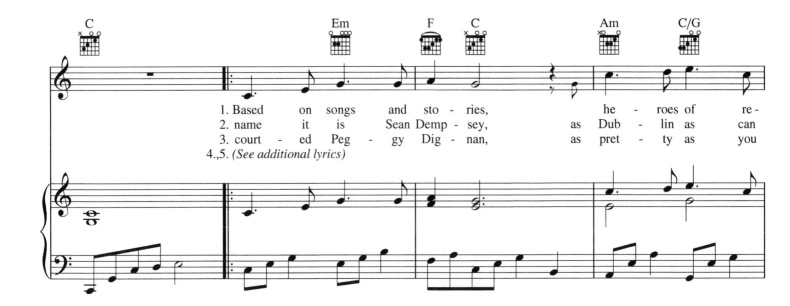

1. Based on songs and sto - ries, he - roes of re -
2. name it is Sean Demp - sey, as Dub - lin as can
3. court - ed Peg - gy Dig - nan, as pret - ty as you
4.,5. *(See additional lyrics)*

nown, _____ are the pass - ing tales and glo - ries, that
be, _____ born hard and late in Pim - li - co, in a
please, _____ a _____ rogue and child of Mar - y from the

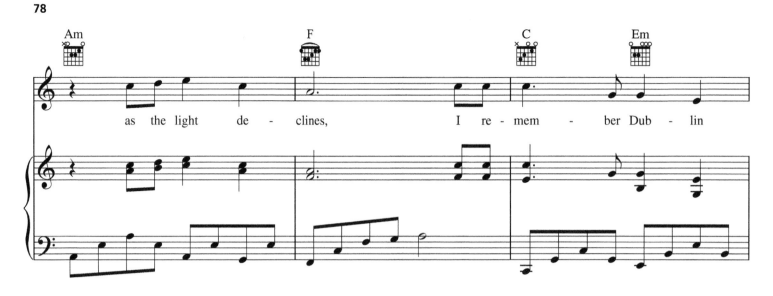

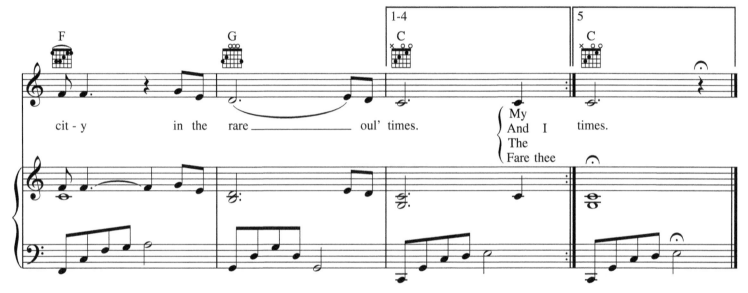

Additional Lyrics

4. The years have made me bitter, the gargle dims my brain,
'Cause Dublin keeps me changing, and nothing seems the same.
The Pillar and the Met have gone, the Royal long since pulled down,
As the great unyielding concrete, makes a city of my town.
Refrain

5. Fare thee well, sweet Anna Liffey, I can no longer stay,
And watch the new glass cages, that spring up along the Quay.
My mind's too full of memories, too old to hear new chimes,
I'm part of what was Dublin, in the rare ould times.
Refrain

THE RISING OF THE MOON

Traditional Irish Folk Song

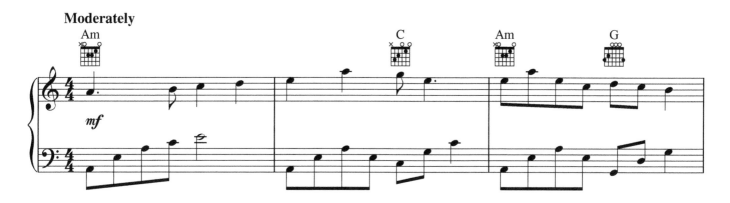

Oh, then tell me, Sean O' - Far - rell,
Oh, then tell me, Sean O' - Far - rell,
Out from man - y a mud - wall cab - in
There be - side the sing - ing riv - er

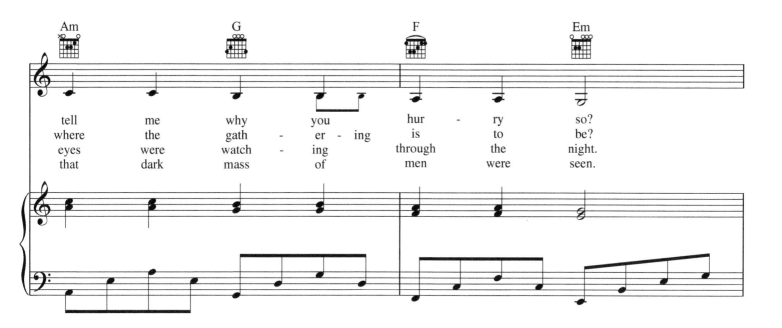

tell me why you hur - ry so?
where the gath - er - ing is to be?
eyes were watch - ing through the night.
that dark mass of men were seen.

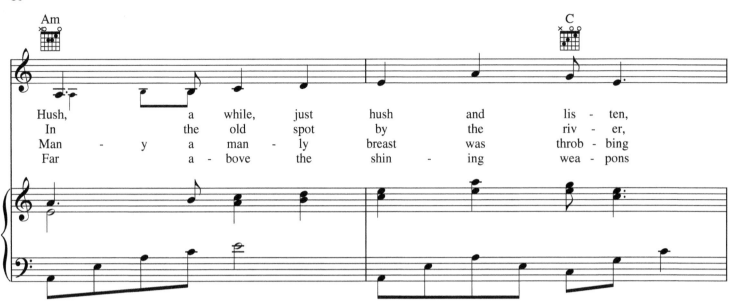

Hush, a while, just hush and lis - ten,
In the old spot by the riv - er,
Man - y a man - ly breast was throb - bing

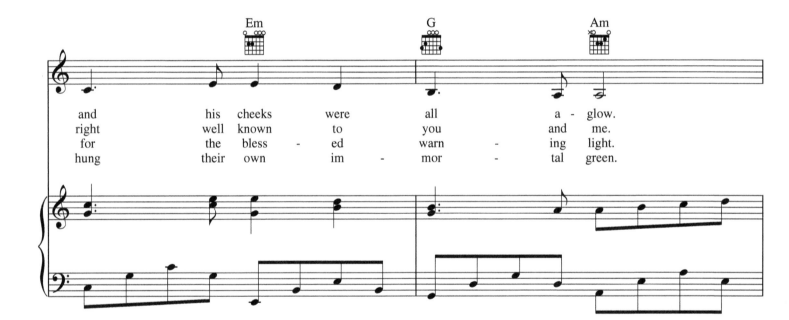

and his cheeks were all a - glow.
right well known to you and me.
for the bless - ed warn - ing light.
hung their own im - mor - tal green.

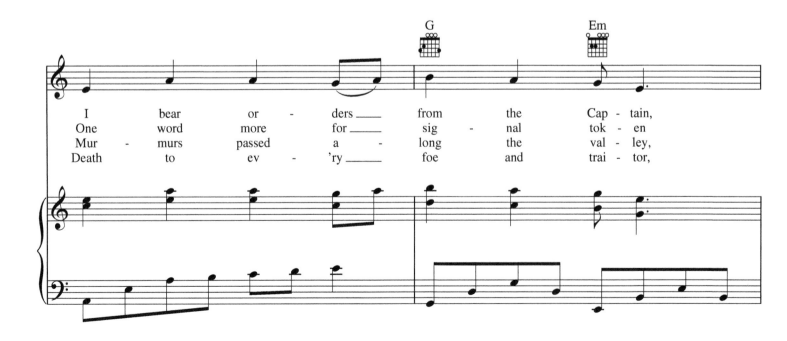

I bear or - ders from the Cap - tain,
One word more for sig - nal tok - en
Mur - murs passed a - long the val - ley,
Death to ev - 'ry foe and trai - tor,

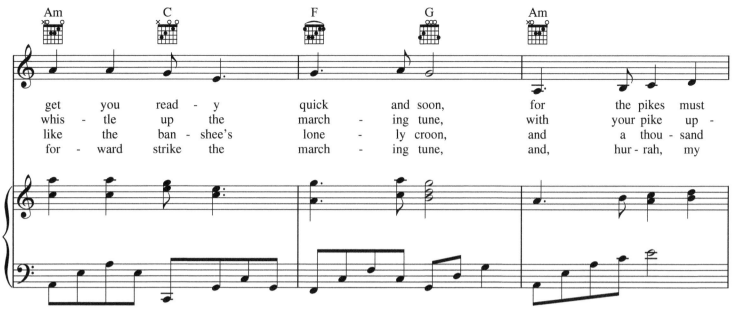

get you read - y quick and soon, for the pikes must
whis - tle up the march - ing tune, with your pike up -
like the ban - shee's lone - ly croon, and a thou - sand
for - ward strike the march - ing tune, and, hur - rah, my

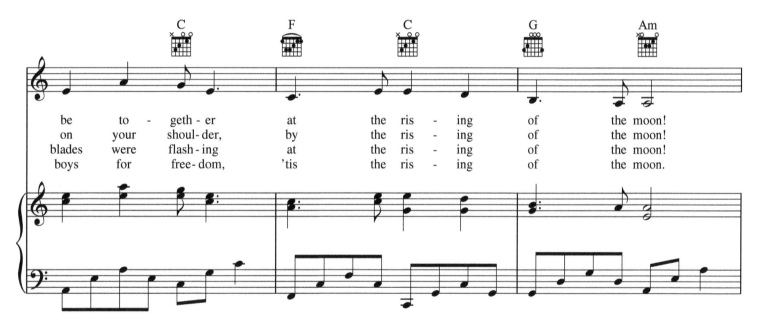

be to - geth - er at the ris - ing of the moon!
on your shoul - der, by the ris - ing of the moon!
blades were flash - ing at the ris - ing of the moon!
boys for free - dom, 'tis the ris - ing of the moon.

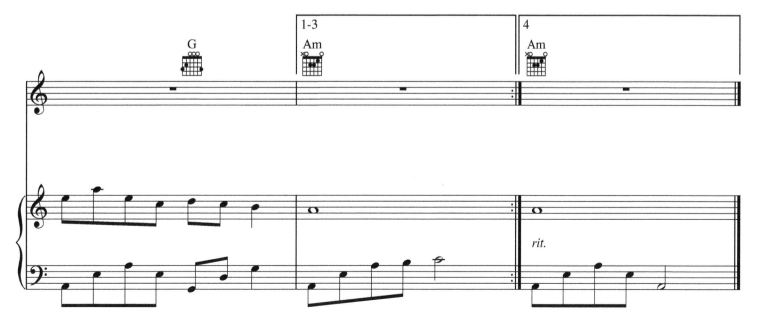

THE ROSE OF TRALEE

Words by C. MORDAUNT SPENCER
Music by CHARLES W. GLOVER

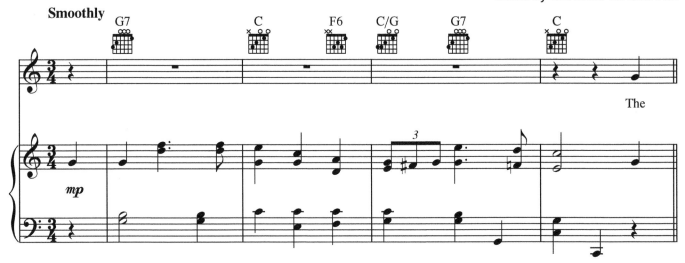

The

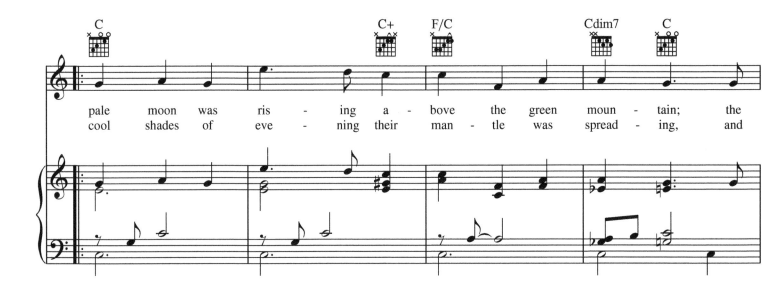

pale moon was ris - ing a - bove the green moun - tain; the
cool shades of eve - ning their man - tle was spread - ing, and

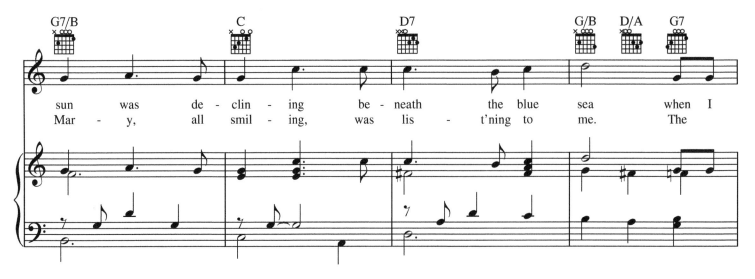

sun was de - clin - ing be - neath the blue sea when I
Mar - y, all smil - ing, was lis - t'ning to me. The

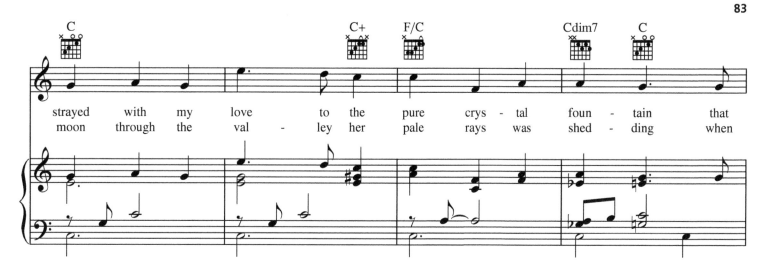

strayed with my love to the pure crys - tal foun - tain that
moon through the val - ley her pale rays was shed - ding that when

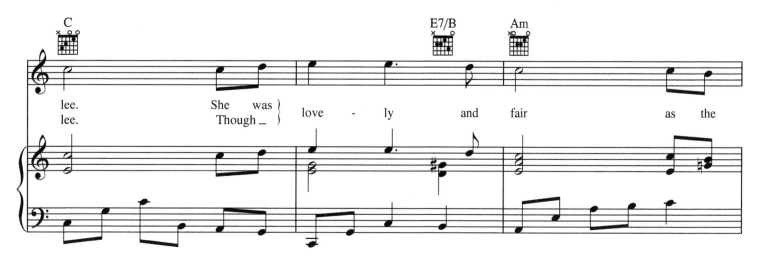

stands in the beau - ti - ful vale of Tra -
I won the heart of the rose of Tra -

lee. She was } love - ly and fair as the
lee. Though __ }

rose of __ the __ sum - mer, yet 'twas not her

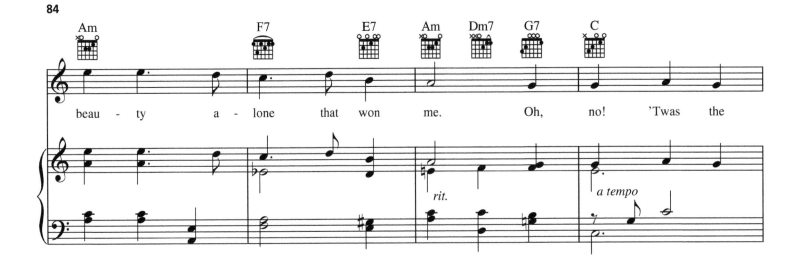

beau-ty a - lone that won me. Oh, no! 'Twas the

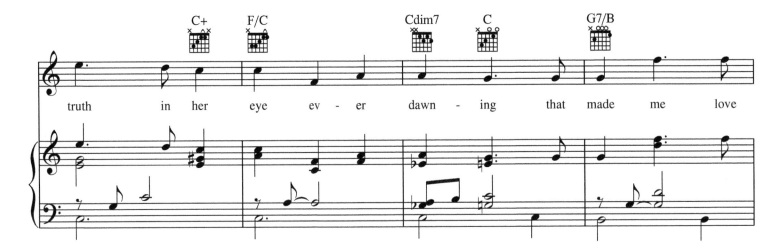

truth in her eye ev - er dawn - ing that made me love

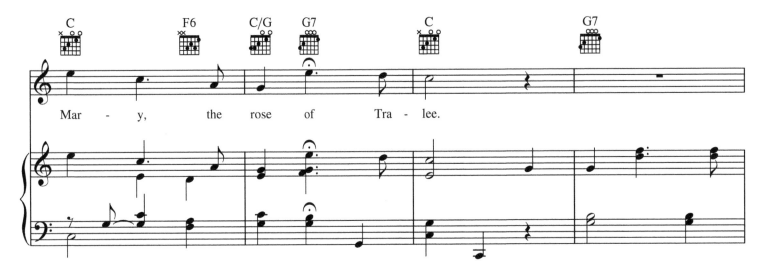

Mar - y, the rose of Tra - lee.

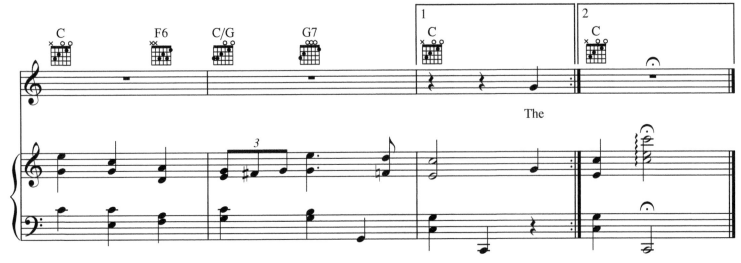

The

ROYAL CANAL

Traditional Irish Folk Song

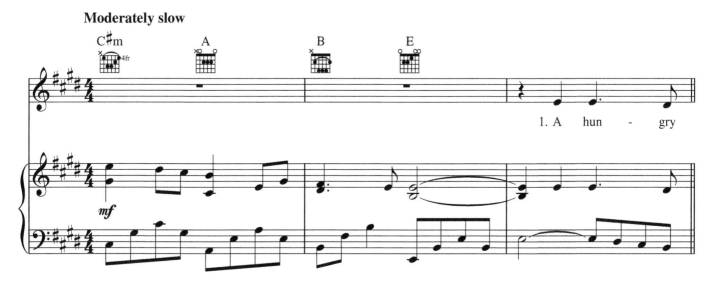

1. A hun - gry

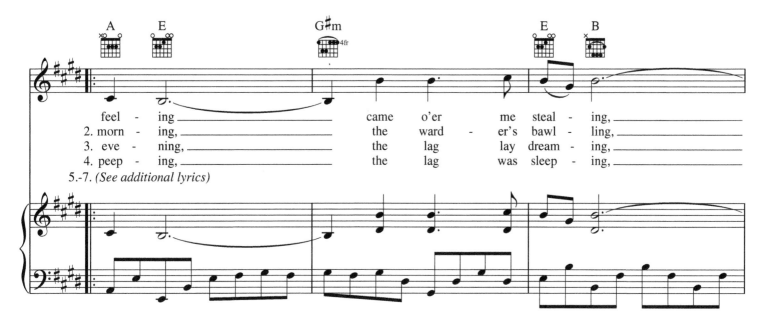

feel - ing _____ came o'er me steal - ing, _____
2. morn - ing, _____ the ward - er's bawl - ling, _____
3. eve - ning, _____ the lag lay dream - ing, _____
4. peep - ing, _____ the lag was sleep - ing, _____
5.-7. (See additional lyrics)

_____ and the mice were squeal - ing in my
_____ "Get _ out of your _ bed and _
_____ the _ sea - gulls wheel - ing high a -
_____ while _ he lay weep - ing for _

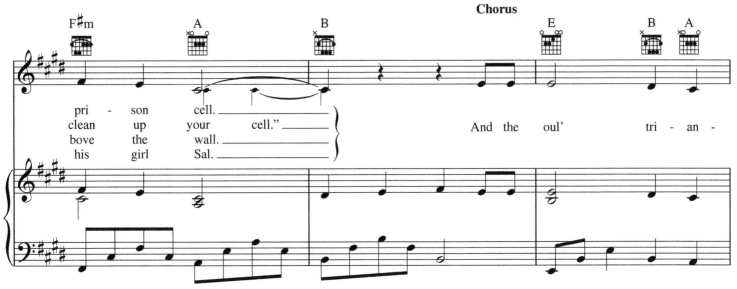

pri - son cell. _____
clean up your cell." _____
bove the wall. _____
his girl Sal. _____

And the oul' tri - an -

gle went jin - gle jan - gle all a -

long the banks of the roy - al can -

Additional Lyrics

5. The wind was rising and the day declining,
   As I lay pining in my prison cell.
   And the ould triangle went jingle jangle
   Along the banks of the Royal Canal.
   Chorus

6. In the female prison there are seventy women.
   I wish it was with them that I did dwell,
   Then that ould triangle could jingle jangle
   Along the banks of the Royal Canal.
   Chorus

7. The day was dying and the wind was sighing,
   As I lay crying in my prison cell.
   And the ould triangle went jingle jangle
   Along the banks of the Royal Canal.
   Chorus

SEVEN DRUNKEN NIGHTS

Traditional Irish Folk Song

1. Well, as I came home on Mon-day night, as drunk as drunk could be, I
2.-5. *(See additional lyrics)*

saw'r a horse out-side the door where my old horse should be. So, I called the wife and I said to her, "Will ya

kind-ly tell to me who owns that horse out-side the door where my old horse should be?"

Chorus

Moderately

Ah, you're drunk, you're drunk, you sil - ly old fool, un - til you can - not see. And

that's a lov - e - ly sow that me moth - er sent to me. Well,

man - y's the day I've trav - eled a hun - dred miles or more, but a

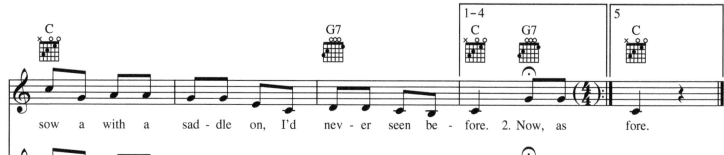

sow a with a sad - dle on, I'd nev - er seen be - fore. 2. Now, as fore.

2. Now, as I came home on Tuesday night,
   As drunk as drunk could be,
   I saw'r a coat behind the door
   Where my old coat should be.
   So I called the wife and I said to her,
   "Will ya kindly tell to me,
   Who owns that coat behind the door
   Where my old coat should be?"

Chorus 2. Ah, you're drunk, you're drunk you silly old fool, till you cannot see.
   That's a lovely blanket that me mother sent to me.
   Well, many's the day I traveled a hundred miles or more,
   But buttons on a blanket sure I never seen before.

3. And as I went home on Wednesday night,
   As drunk as drunk could be,
   I saw'r a pipe upon the chair
   Where my old pipe should be.
   I calls the wife and I says to her,
   "Will ya kindly tell to me,
   Who owns that pipe upon the chair
   Where my old pipe should be?"

Chorus 3. Ah, you're drunk, you're drunk you silly old fool, still you cannot see.
   And that's a lovely tin whistle that me mother sent to me.
   Well, and many's the day I've traveled a hundred miles or more,
   But tobacco in a tin whistle sure I never seen before.

4. And as I went home on Thursday night,
   As drunk as drunk could be,
   I saw'r two boots beneath the bed
   Where my two boots should be.
   I called the wife and I said to her,
   "Will ya kindly tell to me,
   Who owns those boots beneath the bed
   Where my old boots should be?"

Chorus 4. Ah, you're drunk, you're drunk you silly old fool, until you cannot see.
   And that's me lovely geranium pots me mother sent to me.
   Well, it's many's the day I've traveled a hundred miles or more,
   But laces on a geranium pot I never seen before.

5. And as I went home on Friday night,
   As drunk as drunk could be,
   I saw'r a head upon the bed
   Where my old head should be.
   So, I called the wife and I said to her,
   "Will ya kindly tell to me,
   Who owns that head upon the bed
   Where my old head should be?"

Chorus 5. Ah, you're drunk, you're drunk you silly old fool, and still you cannot see.
   That's a baby boy that me mother sent to me.
   Hey, it's many's the day I've traveled a hundred miles or more,
   But a baby boy with whiskers on I never seen before.

TWENTY-ONE YEARS

Traditional Irish Folk Song

1. The Judge said: Stand
2. hear the train
3. months have gone
4.,5. (See additional lyrics)

up,   lad,   and   dry   up   your
com - ing,   'twill   be   up   here   at
by,   love,   I   wish   I   were

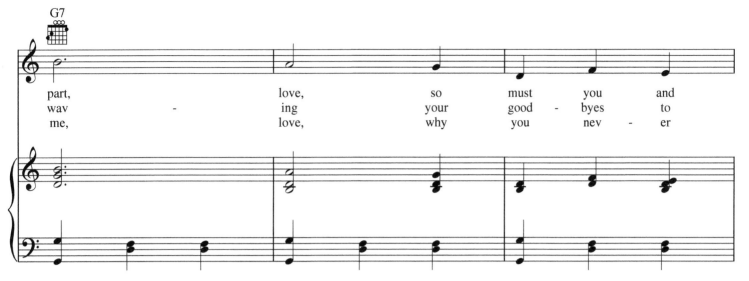

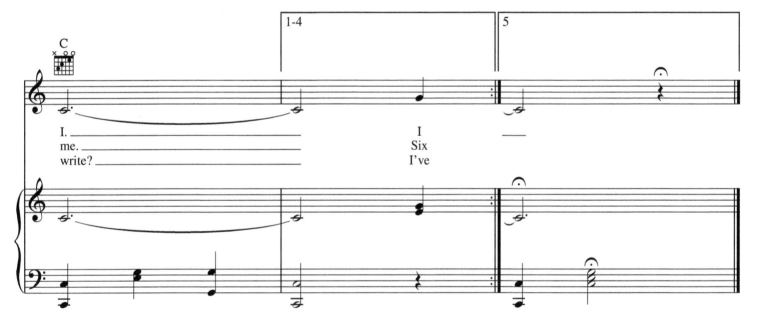

Additional Lyrics

4. I've counted the days, love, I've counted the nights,
   I've counted the footsteps, I've counted the lights,
   I've counted the raindrops, I've counted the stars,
   I've counted a million of these prison bars.

5. I've waited, I've trusted, I've longed for the day,
   A lifetime, so lonely, now my hair's turning grey.
   My thoughts are for you, love, till I'm out of my mind,
   For twenty-one years is a mighty long time.

SPANCIL HILL

Traditional Irish Folk Song

1. Last night as I lay dream-ing of pleas-ant days gone by, me mind bein' bent on ram-bling to Ire-land I did fly. I
2. light-ed with the nov-el-ty, en-chant-ed with the scene, where in my ear-ly boy-hood where of-ten I had been. I
3. be-ing the twen-ty third of June, the day be-fore the fair, when Ire-land's sons and daugh-ters in crowds as-sem-bled there. The

4.-6. *(See additional lyrics)*

Additional Lyrics

4. I went to see my neighbors, to hear what they might say,
   The old ones were all dead and gone, the others turning grey.
   I met with tailor Quigley, he's as bold as ever still,
   Sure he used to make my britches when I lived in Spancil Hill.

5. I paid a flying visit to my first and only love,
   She's white as any lily and gentle as a dove.
   She threw her arms around me, saying, "Johnny, I love you still."
   She's Mag, the farmer's daughter and the pride of Spancil Hill.

6. I dreamt I stooped and kissed her as in the days of yore.
   She said, "Johnny, you're only joking, as many's the time before."
   The cock crew in the morning, he crew both loud and shrill,
   And I woke in California, many miles from Spancil Hill.

THE STONE OUTSIDE DAN MURPHY'S DOOR

Traditional Irish Folk Song

Moderately fast

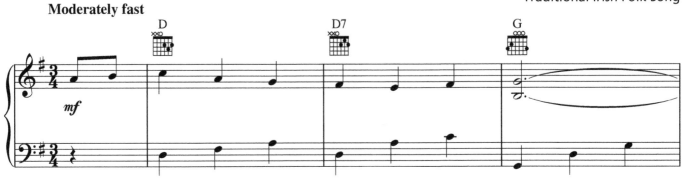

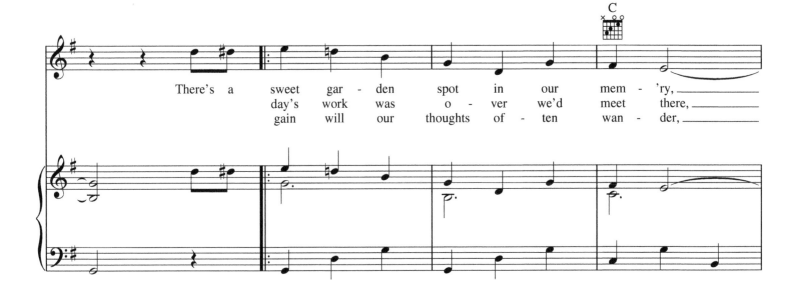

There's a sweet gar - den spot in our mem - 'ry, _____
day's work was o - ver we'd meet there, _____
gain will our thoughts of - ten wan - der, _____

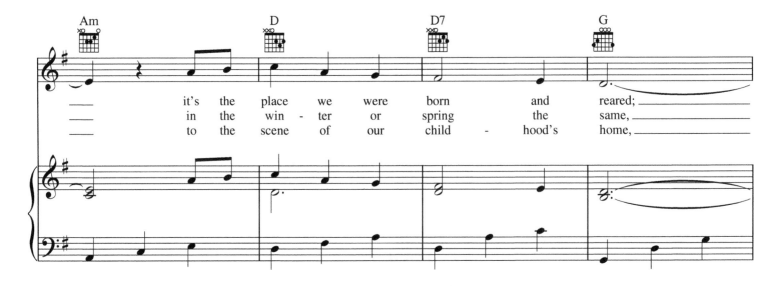

it's the place we were born and reared; _____
in the win - ter or spring the same, _____
to the scene of our child - hood's home, _____

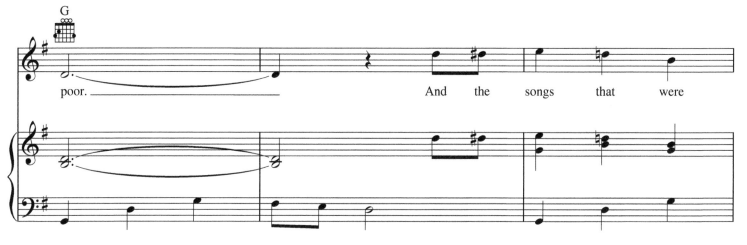

poor. _____ And the songs that were

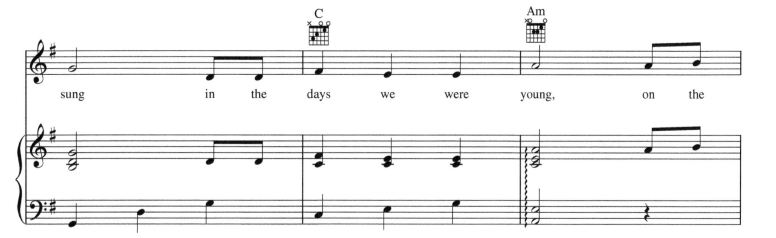

sung in the days we were young, on the

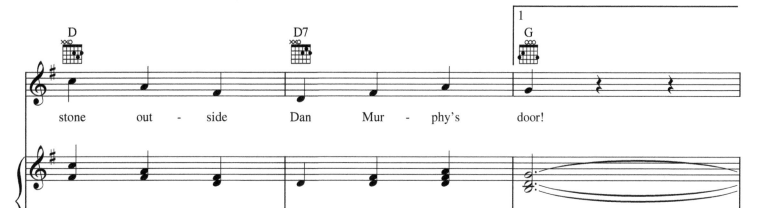

stone out - side Dan Mur - phy's door!

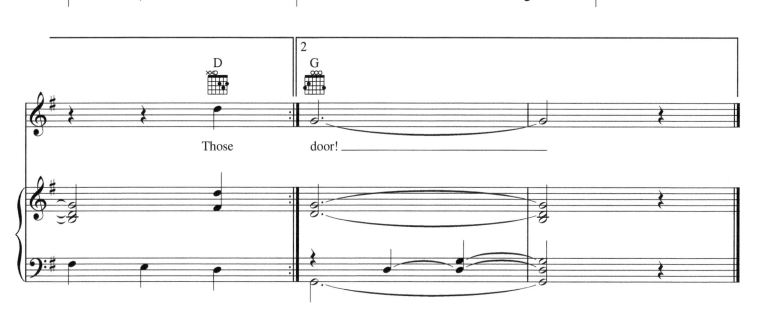

Those door! _____

THE WAXIES DARGLE

Traditional Irish Folk Song

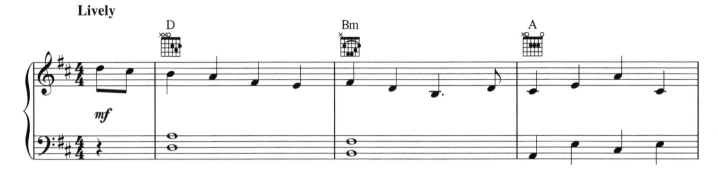

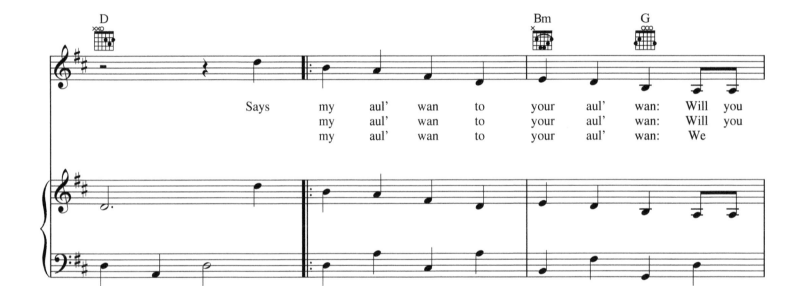

Says my aul' wan to your aul' wan: Will you
my aul' wan to your aul' wan: Will you
my aul' wan to your aul' wan: We

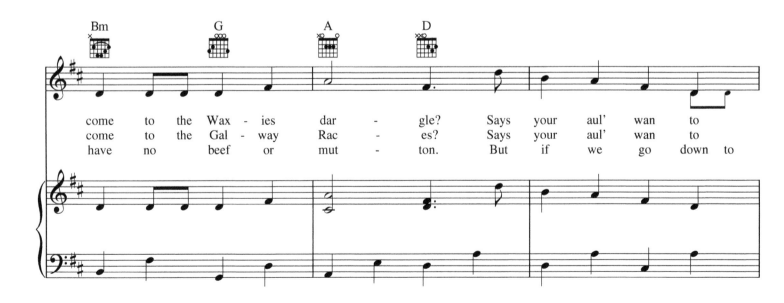

come to the Wax - ies dar - gle? Says your aul' wan to
come to the Gal - way Rac - es? Says your aul' wan to
have no beef or mut - ton. But if we go down to

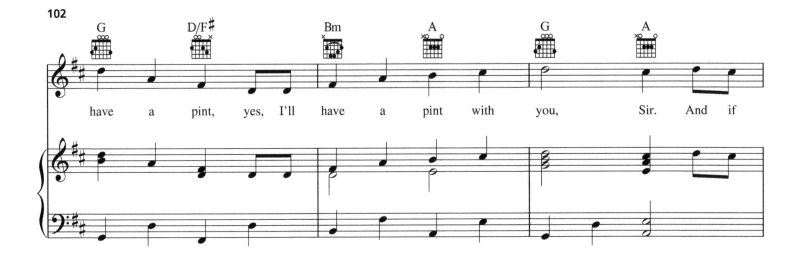

have a pint, yes, I'll have a pint with you, Sir. And if

one of ya does-n't or - der soon, we'll be thrown out of the

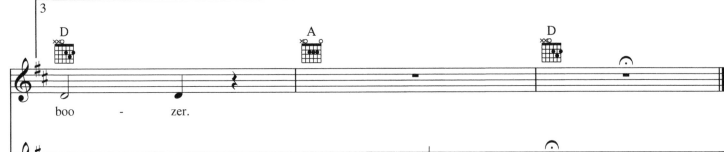

1, 2

boo - zer.

{ Says
{ Says

3

boo - zer.

WHISKEY, YOU'RE THE DEVIL

Traditional Irish Folk Song

Whis-key you're the dev-il, _____ you're lead-in' me a-stray, o-ver hills and moun-tains and to A-mer-i-cae. You're sweet-er, strong-er, de-cent-er, you're

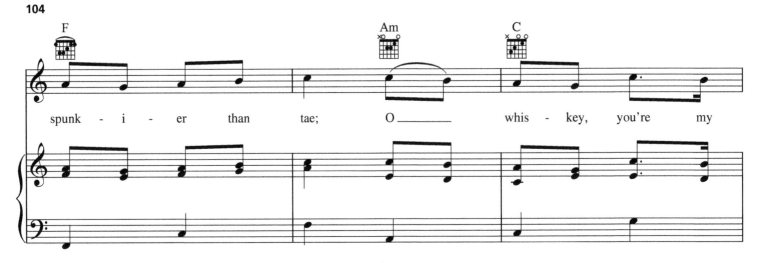

spunk - i - er than tae; O _____ whis - key, you're my

To Coda ⊕

dar - lin' drunk or so - ber.
Oh, now, brave boys, we're
The French are fight - ing
Said the moth - er, "So not

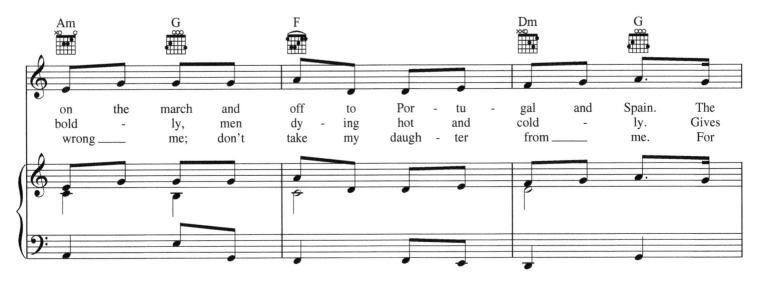

on the march and off to Por - tu - gal and Spain. The
bold - ly, men dy - ing hot and cold - ly. Gives
wrong ____ me; don't take my daugh - ter from ____ me. For

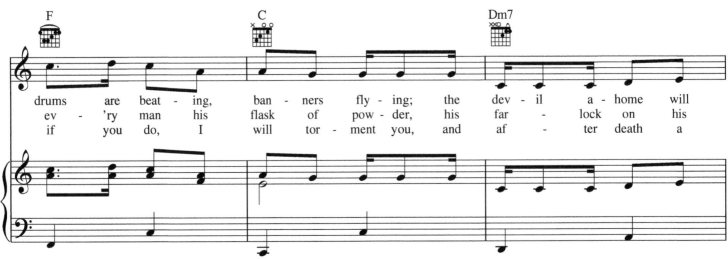

drums are beat - ing, ban - ners fly - ing; the dev - il a - home will
ev - 'ry man his flask of pow - der, his far - lock on his
if you do, I will tor - ment you, and af - ter death a

WHISKEY IN THE JAR

Traditional Irish Folk Song

1. As

I was go - in' o - ver the Cork and Ker - ry moun - tains,
2. count - ed out his mon - ey; paid a pret - ty pen - ny.
3. ear - ly in the morn - ing, be - fore I rose to trav - el.
4. *(See additional lyrics)*

met with Cap - tain Far - rell and his mon - ey he was count - in'.
Put it in me pock - et and I took it home to Jen - ny.
Up rides a band of foot - men and like - wise rash - er Far - rell.

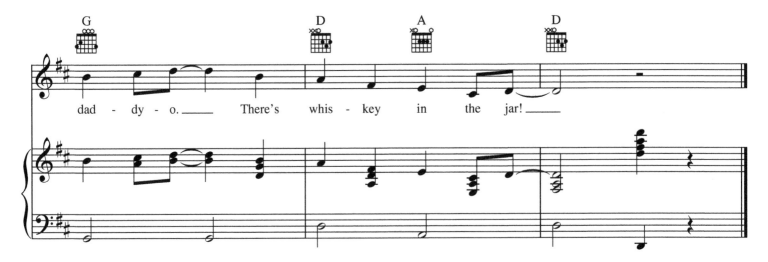

Additional Lyrics

4. Some take delight in the fishin' and the fowlin'.
Others take delight in the carriage gently rollin'.
Ah, but I take delight in the juice of the barley;
Courtin' pretty women in the mountains of Killarney.
Musha ring dumma doo-rama da.
Chorus

WILD ROVER

Traditional Irish Folk Song

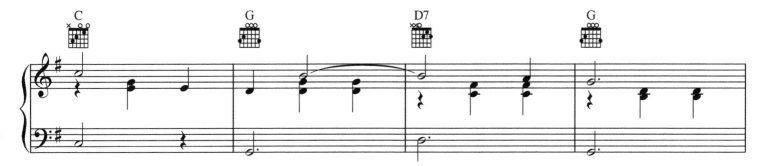

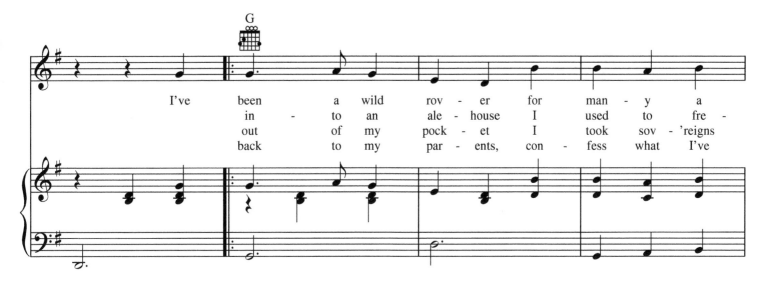

I've been a wild rov - er for man - y a
in - to an ale - house I used to fre -
out of my pock - et I took sov - 'reigns
back to my par - ents, con - fess what I've

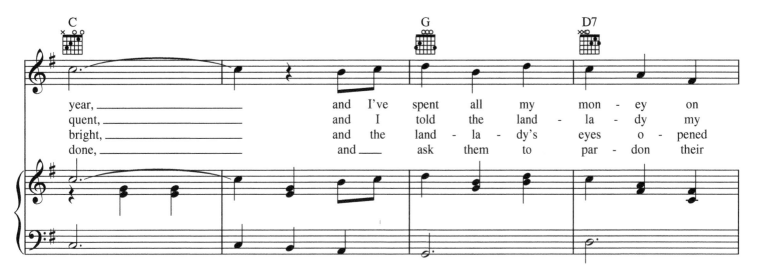

year, _____ and I've spent all my mon - ey on
quent, _____ and I told the land - la - dy my
bright, _____ and the land - la - dy's eyes o - pened
done, _____ and ___ ask them to par - don their

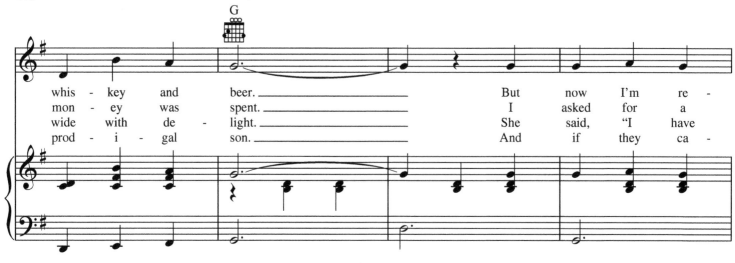

whis - key and beer. _____ But now I'm re - a -
mon - ey was spent. _____ I asked for a
wide with de - light. _____ She said, "I have
prod - i - gal son. _____ And if they ca -

turn - ing with gold in great store, _____ and I
bot - tle; she an - swered me, "Nay, _____ such a
whis - kies and wines of the best, _____ and the
ress me as oft - times be - fore, _____ then I

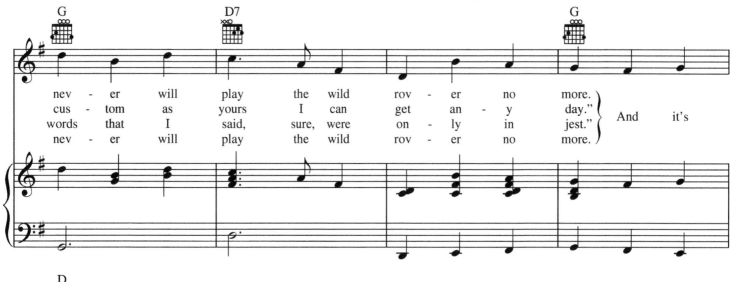

nev - er will play the wild rov - er no more.
cus - tom as yours I can get an - y day." And it's
words that I said, sure, were on - ly in jest."
nev - er will play the wild rov - er no more.

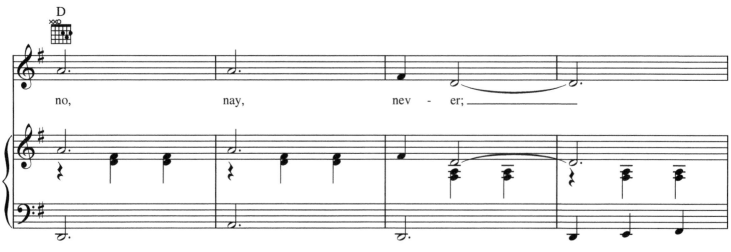

no, nay, nev - er; _____

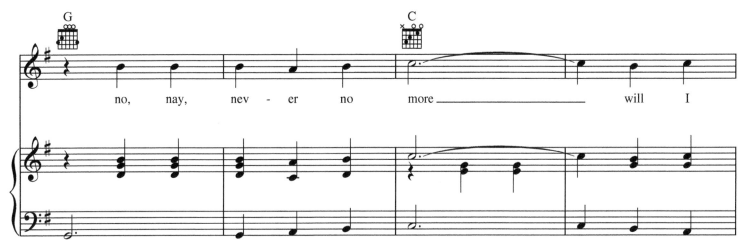

no, nay, nev - er no more _____ will I

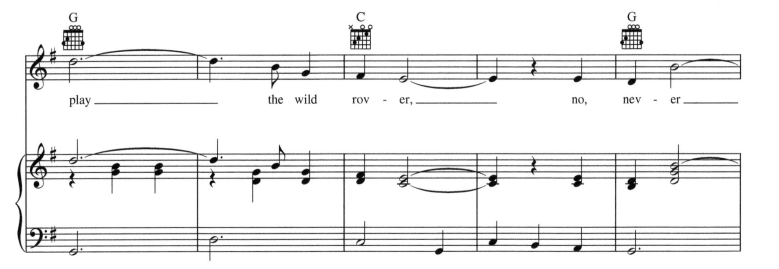

play _____ the wild rov - er, _____ no, nev - er _____

_____ no more. _____

{ I went
Then _____ more.
I'll go

more Celtic & Irish songbooks

The popularity of Celtic music has soared over the last decade
due to the resurgence of folk instruments, Celtic dancing, and Irish culture overall.

Learn how to play these beloved songs with these great songbooks!

THE BEST OF IRISH MUSIC

80 of the best Irish songs ever written in one comprehensive collection. Includes: Danny Boy • If I Knock the "L" out of Kelly • Macnamara's Band • Molly Malone • My Wild Irish Rose • Peg o' My Heart • Too-Ra-Loo-Ra-Loo-Ral (That's an Irish Lullaby) • Wearin' of the Green • When Irish Eyes Are Smiling • and more.
00315064 P/V/G $16.95

THE BIG BOOK OF IRISH SONGS

A great collection of 75 beloved Irish tunes, from folk songs to Tin Pan Alley favorites! Includes: Erin! Oh Erin! • Father O'Flynn • Finnegan's Wake • I'll Take You Home Again, Kathleen • The Irish Rover • The Irish Washerwoman • Jug of Punch • Kerry Dance • Who Threw the Overalls in Mrs. Murphy's Chowder • Wild Rover • and more.
00310981 P/V/G $19.95

THE CELTIC COLLECTION

The Phillip Keveren Series

Features 15 traditional Irish folk tunes masterfully arranged in Celtic style by the incomparable Phillip Keveren. Songs include: Be Thou My Vision • The Galway Piper • Kitty of Coleraine • The Lark in the Clear Air • Molly Malone (Cockles & Mussels) • and more.
00310549 Piano Solo $12.95

THE GRAND IRISH SONGBOOK

125 cherished folk songs, including: Believe Me, If All Those Endearing Young Charms • The Croppy Boy • Danny Boy • The Galway Races • Johnny, I Hardly Knew You • Jug of Punch • My Wild Irish Rose • Too-Ra-Loo-Ra-Loo-Ral (That's an Irish Lullaby) • The Wearing of the Green • When Irish Eyes Are Smiling • and more.
00311320 P/V/G $19.95

IRISH BALLADS

Nearly 60 traditional Irish ballads, including: Black Velvet Band • Brennan on the Moor • Cliffs of Doneen • Down by the Sally Gardens • I Know My Love • I Never Will Marry • Johnny, I Hardly Knew You • Leaving of Liverpool • Minstrel Boy • Red Is the Rose • When You Were Sweet Sixteen • Wild Rover • and more.
00311322 P/V/G $14.95

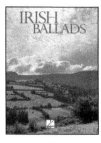

IRISH FAVORITES

From sentimental favorites to happy-go-lucky singalongs, this songbook celebrates the Irish cultural heritage of music. 30 songs, including: Danny Boy (Londonderry Air) • The Girl I Left Behind Me • Killarney • My Wild Irish Rose • Tourelay • Who Threw the Overalls in Mistress Murphy's Chowder • and more!
00311615 P/V/G...$10.95

IRISH PUB SONGS

Grab a pint and this songbook for an evening of Irish fun! 40 songs, including: All for Me Grog • The Fields of Athenry • I Never Will Marry • I'm a Rover and Seldom Sober • The Irish Rover • Jug of Punch • Leaving of Liverpool • A Nation Once Again • The Rare Ould Times • Whiskey in the Jar • Whiskey, You're the Devil • and more.
00311321 P/V/G $12.95

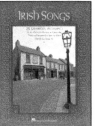

IRISH SONGS

25 traditional favorites, including: At the Ball of Kirriemuir • At the End of the Rainbow • Dear Old Donegal • Galway Bay • Hannigan's Hooley • The Isle of Innisfree • It's the Same Old Shillelagh • The Moonshiner • The Spinning Wheel • The Whistling Gypsy • Will Ye Go, Lassie, Go • and more.
00311323 P/V/G $12.95

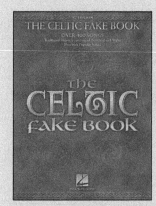

THE CELTIC FAKE BOOK

This amazing collection assembles over 400 songs from Ireland, Scotland and Wales – complete with Gaelic lyrics where applicable – and a pronunciation guide. Titles include: Across the Western Ocean • Along with My Love I'll Go • Altar Isle o' the Sea • Auld Lang Syne • Avondale • The Band Played On • Barbara Allen • Blessing of the Road • The Blue Bells of Scotland • The Bonniest Lass • A Bunch of Thyme • The Chanty That Beguiled the Witch • Columbus Was an Irishman • Danny Boy • Duffy's Blunders • Erin! Oh Erin! • Father Murphy • Finnegan's Wake • The Galway Piper • The Girl I Left Behind Me • Has Anybody Here Seen Kelly • I Know Where I'm Goin' • Irish Rover • Loch Lomond • My Bonnie Lies over the Ocean • The Shores of Amerikay • The Sons of Liberty • Who Threw the Overalls in Mistress Murphy's Chowder • and hundreds more. Also includes many Irish popular songs as a bonus.
00240153 Melody/Lyrics/Chords $25.00

FOR MORE INFORMATION, SEE YOUR LOCAL MUSIC DEALER,
OR WRITE TO:

HAL•LEONARD®
CORPORATION
7777 W. BLUEMOUND RD. P.O. BOX 13819 MILWAUKEE, WI 53213

Visit Hal Leonard Online at www.halleonard.com

Prices, contents and availability subject to change without notice.

0116